Local Government Records

Local Government Records

An Introduction to Their Management, Preservation, and Use

H. G. Jones

American Association for State and Local History
Nashville, Tennessee

Author and publisher make grateful acknowledgment to the sources listed below for permission to use in this book the illustrations specified.
The New York State Archives, State Education Department of New York, for Figs. 1 and 22.
Records of Suffolk County, Massachusetts, Colonial Court Records Project, Boston, Massachusetts, and the *Boston Bar Journal* for Figs. 2, 29, and 30.
The Society of American Archivists and the *American Archivist* for Fig. 3.
The Oregon State Archives Division for Fig. 4.
The Ohio Historical Society for Figs. 6 and 11.
The North Carolina Collection and the North Carolina Division of Archives and History, University of North Carolina at Chapel Hill, for Figs. 7, 8, 9, 13, 14, 16, 26, 27, and 28.
Records Section, Multnomah County, Oregon, for Fig. 10.
Records Management, City of Portland, Oregon, for Fig. 12.
William Benedon, author of *Records Management* (Los Angeles: Trident Bookstore, UCLA, 1973), for Figs. 15, 17, and 21.
National Micrographics Association for Fig. 18.
Modern Office Procedures, Public Affairs Division, Rockwell International, for Figs. 23, 24, and 25.

Library of Congress Cataloguing-in-Publication Data

Jones, Houston Gwynne, 1924-
Local government records, an introduction to their management, preservation, and use.

Includes bibliographical references and index.
1. Archives—United States—Management. 2. Public records—United States. 3. United States—Politics and government—Sources. I. American Association for State and Local History. II. Title.
CD3024.J66 352'.16'40973 79-24743
ISBN 0-910050-42-2

Research for and publication of this book was made possible by a grant from the National Historical Publications and Records Commission.

Contents

Part 1: Management and Preservation

Part 2: Use of Local Government Records

Illustrations

Preface

GROUND was broken in 1936 in Wisconsin for the new town of Greendale, one of the first three "Greenbelt" communities sponsored by the federal government as an experiment in housing. Two years later, the first houses were occupied. By 1941—just five years after the first spade of dirt was turned—there were 635 houses in Greendale. In addition, the young municipality had produced 103 separate series of records so diverse that the Historical Records Survey required 84 single-spaced typewritten pages just to describe them and place them in their organizational setting.

Those simple facts are cited here as a twentieth-century illustration of how naturally, quickly, and voluminously public records are generated by a local governmental unit. The management, preservation, and use of local public records are the subjects of this book.

Upon the expiration of my term as president of the Society of American Archivists in 1969, I chided my colleagues for having solved too few of the problems that existed at the time of the founding of the organization more than three decades earlier. I pointed out that subjects of sessions at our annual meetings often were identical to those discussed repeatedly over the years—a reliable indication that problems remained unsolved. By substituting "a family conversation around the dinner table" for the traditional presidential address, I sought to focus on our mediocre record of accomplishment as a means of goading my colleagues into bolder leadership in the future.

When, nearly a decade later, the American Association for State and Local History invited me to review the status of local government records in the United States and to write this book, I accepted partially because the project would allow me to measure progress made in the field of local public records since my earlier dismal assessment. That the progress had been substantial I had little reason to doubt, for already, in the decade of the '60s, several states had developed local records programs that appeared to offer vigorous leadership and professional assistance to help solve the problems of counties and municipalities. Furthermore, revolutionary new machine-readable record-keeping systems promised virtually to eliminate paper as a recording medium, creating, to be sure, new problems, but at least minimizing those of bulk and accessibility. Microfilm was already a proven medium, but its coupling with computers offered great hope that public offices might become as aseptic and efficient as the local bank.

My subsequent observations in eight states and correspondence with state and local officials in the forty-two others have failed to justify my optimism, for progress in records management at the local level has been minimal throughout the nation. True, during the past decade, several states have strengthened their archival and records management services to counties and municipalities, but they remain in the minority; furthermore, the vitality of programs in some states that had pioneered in comprehensive services appears to have waned. Some counties and cities have, with or without state encouragement, developed programs of varying effectiveness, and several of these are cited in this book. On the other hand, a number of local governments that earlier launched much-publicized programs appear to have lost their original vigor.

There are several causes for the disappointing status of local government records management. Only in rare instances have archivists and records managers been willing to go into the counties and municipalities and skillfully lobby the halls of the legislature in the cause of improved records management programs. Their organizations have shown little stomach for the intensive, unglamorous grass-roots campaigns necessary to elicit public support for professional programs. Local officials and their organizations have been caught up in policy issues and externally imposed programs and regulations, leaving them little time and energy to devote to routine problems such as records management. In short, professional records management is unknown to thousands of local government jurisdictions in the United States because it does not occupy a high priority among archivists, records managers, state and local officials, and their respective organizations.

The original objective of this study—to provide something of a manual for the management and use of local records, including the outline of a "model" local records program—was abandoned early in the nationwide survey when it became evident that there exists in the country neither a model program nor an agreement on what should constitute a model program. In the first place, there are in the neighborhood of 81,000 local government units in the United States, each a subdivision of the state in which it is located and with such powers as have been granted to it by the state constitution or legislative acts. The pattern is different in each of the fifty states. In the second place, state laws relating to local records differ; accordingly, while a few state archival agencies provide rather broad services to counties and municipalities, most provide only advice or a minimum of assistance. Some provide no leadership. Even in states with reasonably good assistance programs, local initiative varies among the thousands of counties and municipalities.

This book, therefore, is not intended as a what-to-do and how-to-do-it manual. Instead, it seeks to provide an *introduction* to the management, preservation, and use of local public records. If it furnishes a better understanding of the need for improved management and more extensive research use of local records, my purpose will have been only partially accomplished, for nothing short of the initiation or strengthening of records management programs across the nation will meet the requirements for more efficient and economical administration of local government and increased utilization of local documentary resources for the advancement of knowledge.

Although Part I deals with subjects of primary concern to the local official, and Part II discusses matters of interest to the researcher, this book is written with the hope that both parts will be read in their entirety. My theme is the community of interest between the local official, who creates and manages the records, and the researcher, who uses the contents of the records to provide greater knowledge of the community and its history. Each complements the work of the other.

I am indebted to many persons for advice and supporting materials in connection with this study. Helpful books and articles generally are cited in the text or footnotes, but one should be mentioned here: the article by David Levine, now of the Martin Luther King, Jr., Center for Social Change, published in the April 1977 issue of *American Archivist* under the title "The Management and Preservation of Local Public Records: Report of the State and Local Records Committee." Cleo A. Hughes of the Tennessee State Library and Archives furnished me with responses to her 1977 questionnaire on archival services to municipalities. An archival official in each state responded to a questionnaire that I circulated in 1978, and many of them provided supplementary information on programs in their states. I must especially acknowledge the assistance of Kenneth L. Brock of the New York State Archives and James D. Porter of the Oregon State Archives, and members of their staffs, who accompanied me to selected courthouses and municipal buildings for firsthand observations and discussions. Among the other officials who facilitated the study in their states were John M. Kinney of the Alaska State Archives, John E. Daly of the Illinois State Archives, Dennis East II and Frank Levstik of the Ohio Historical Society, David B. Gracy II and Marilyn VonKohl of the Texas State Archives, and Sidney F. McAlpin and Michael S. Saunders of the Washington Division of Archives and Records Management. In my home state, I drew upon the expertise of my successors, Thornton W. Mitchell and Frank D. Gatton of the North Carolina Division of Archives and History.

Influential in my decision to undertake this project were the memories of fine working relationships with state and county officials who in 1959 joined me in persuading the North Carolina General Assembly to authorize a bold new statewide records management assistance program for the counties and municipalities of the state—people like Betty June Hayes, former president of the National Association of County Recorders and Clerks; William G. Massey, register of deeds for Johnston County; D. M. McLelland, clerk of court in Alamance County; J. Alexander McMahon, former executive secretary of the Association of County Commissioners; Senator Sam M. Bason and Representatives Edward H. Wilson and J. Toliver Davis, who sponsored the bills in the legislature; and Rear Admiral Alex M. Patterson (USN, Ret.), who for a dozen years effectively and harmoniously administered the program under the eye of a former sailor whose rank never exceeded yeoman second class. To them, and to many others who supplied assistance, information, suggestions, or encouragement, I am grateful.

The book was made possible by a grant from the National Historical Publications and Records Commission to the American Association for State and Local History; in other words, it was financed from the pockets of the American taxpayers. I hold the perhaps immodest hope that the cost of the grant will be returned to the citizens manyfold through the encouragement of more efficient and economical records management programs in the counties and municipalities of the nation.

H. G. Jones

Chapel Hill, North Carolina
June 1979

Part 1

Management and Preservation

1

Records Management in Perspective

Background

NEARLY a century and a half ago, a New Englander, Richard Bartlett, wrote, "To provide for the safe and perfect keeping of the Public Archives, is so obviously one of the first and most imperative duties of a legislature, that no argument could make it plainer to a reflecting mind."[1] Many years later, another New Englander, Waldo Gifford Leland, added, "The chief monument of the history of a nation is its archives, the preservation of which is recognized by all civilized countries as a natural and proper function of government."[2]

Bartlett was referring to state records, Leland to the records of the federal government. Oddly, there is not in the English language an equally popular quotation rationalizing the preservation of the records of local governments. Indeed, except for a few specialized studies relating to local records in particular communities, literature on the subject is virtually nonexistent. Perhaps it is because local records are so close at hand, so familiar to local people, and so personal in their content that historians and other researchers have taken for granted their justification and their security. Perhaps also the assumption by state and federal governments of many responsibilities formerly exercised by local governments has obscured the continuing significance of local

1. Richard G. Wood, "Richard Bartlett, Minor Archival Prophet," *American Archivist* 17 (January 1954): 14. Bartlett, secretary of state of New Hampshire, conducted one of the earliest surveys of archives in the United States.

2. Waldo G. Leland, "The National Archives: A Programme," *American Historical Review* 18 (October 1912): 1. Leland, longtime director of the American Council of Learned Societies, was a leading proponent of the establishment of the National Archives.

records. No longer is the individual citizen's contact with government limited to periodic visits to the county courthouse or town or city hall. The long arms of the state and federal governments reach directly to him through tax collections, law enforcement, highway construction and maintenance, educational institutions, welfare programs, and regulations of a seemingly infinite variety.

The inattention of the literature to local records certainly cannot be blamed upon the paucity of sources, for the legislative journals of the colonies and states are rich in evidence that, from the formation of governments in America, the creation and preservation of local records have been of vital concern. Usually one of the first acts of governments was the setting aside of public land for "Court howses & howses for publique meetings" and the appointment of one or more officers to "keep exact entries in fair books of all public affairs of the said Counties. . . ."[3] Whether proprietary or royal, colonies were concerned particularly with the proper recording of land titles as a means of assessing and collecting quitrents and of protecting property rights. In addition, local officials were usually responsible for the settlement of estates, the recording of vital statistics, the conduct of county and town government, and the general administration of justice. Few citizens needed recourse to a higher level of government.

Still, despite statutory provisions for adequate record-keeping at the local level, these same legislative journals reveal the inadequacy of their enforcement, for bills introduced into the assembly were usually corrective in nature rather than commendatory. The most frequent complaints contained in preambles involved the negligence of officials, the absence of fixed courthouses and consequent scattering of public records in private hands, and the destruction of records by fire or other calamity. Probably typical of the problems of other colonies and states were these reports in North Carolina: In 1714 it was recorded that "by misfortune of the War in this Government with the Indians, the office of the . . . Precinct of Craven [was] burnt"; a bill during the Confederation period complained of "the frequent removal of County records from one place to another upon the alteration of Clerks and the inattention of Clerks of the County Courts" and sought to require each clerk to record papers "in books by him to be kept for that purpose well bound"; a few years later another act observed that "the records of the

3. Quoted in H. G. Jones, *For History's Sake: The Preservation and Publication of North Carolina History, 1663–1903* (Chapel Hill: University of North Carolina Press, 1966), pp. 4, 6.

registers office in the counties of Orange and Tyrrel [*sic*] are in a ruinous situation, occasioned by being removed at sundry times during the late war" and ordered that the records be transcribed. In the same state, at least forty fires destroyed county records between 1794 and 1900; and during another period of four decades, officials in thirty-three counties were ordered by the General Assembly to return their offices to the county seats or to within specified distances of the courthouses. All told, fire and the dispersal of records outside government buildings probably resulted in the loss of more records than any other cause except negligence.[4]

Fig. 1. Fire, a traditional enemy of records, has not been completely eliminated even by modern buildings. Pictured here, local records in New York were seriously damaged by fire, heat, and water. (New York State Archives)

The frequency of these legislative acts is explained by the absence of effective colonywide and later statewide legislation governing local records, for, prior to the last quarter of the nineteenth century, there was no administrative structure in any state that regularly monitored the conditions of records in the counties, towns, and cities. Standards for the care of their records, therefore, were left to the discretion of the

4. Jones, *For History's Sake,* pp. 21, 73–74, 119.

local officials except when acts were passed by the legislature ordering specific improvements.

Changing Formats

Although the management of records in America has been complicated by their changing composition and formats, we can be grateful that the establishment of the colonies came at a time when certain European record-keeping practices were on the wane. Neither the complex English registry system nor the use of animal skins as a writing surface became common in the colonies; consequently, records problems in America have been limited—until recently—to paper materials.

From the earliest days in the English colonies, the most important records were entered in bound books. In 1665, for instance, the "Concessions and Agreement" between the Lords Proprietors and Major William Yeamans of the ill-fated Cape Fear colony required the secretary to ". . . keep exact entries in fair books of all public affairs of the said Counties. . . ." Thus minutes, deeds, wills, court decisions, and outgoing (and sometimes incoming) letters were laboriously copied into books. It was to the books (which were usually indexed) that reference was made. This method of hand-copying of records directly onto book paper continued into the twentieth century, and a mark of dignity of a county or municipal office was the display of leather-bound, hand-tooled volumes on expensive, metal, roller-type shelving. Although a system of "press-copying" was often used for correspondence during the nineteenth century, that method fortunately was not adopted widely for recording official documents.

So long as record books were made of durable paper, they posed few problems, except for the occasional fading of inferior ink and the need for recopying and/or rebinding heavily used volumes. The substitution of acidic paper after the Civil War, however, introduced a serious threat, and bound volumes for the period of, roughly, 1870 to 1900 sometimes deteriorated rapidly. Fortunately, manufacturers of paper soon recognized the necessity of using a high grade of rag paper for record books, and the problem was ameliorated in the twentieth century.

The adoption of typewritten in lieu of handwritten transcriptions and the later development of photographic copying methods, of which Photostat was the most prominent, resulted in the binding of loose sheets, often into expensive leather binders. By the 1950s, another

Fig. 2. County records of the colonial era consisted of "file papers"—folded two or three times and wrapped with ribbon—and books into which abstracts of the file papers were copied. (Records of Suffolk County, Massachusetts. Courtesy of Gabrielle Keller)

copying technique had been adopted rather widely: that of microfilming the original documents, making enlarged paper copies from the microfilm images, and binding the enlargements. The advantage of both types of photographic recording lay in the production of a replica of the original, including exact wording and signatures; their disadvantages sometimes included the negative-reading quality (i.e., white lettering on black background) and the instability of the images when not properly exposed and washed.

While the copying of documentation into bound books provided convenient access to information, there was a concomitant adverse effect upon the original documents, which, once their contents had been recorded in books, were usually folded, wrapped with a string, and relegated to closets and storerooms. Filing equipment was virtually unknown prior to the Civil War, but sometimes the bundled records were placed on shelves and in boxes, chests, and barrels. These original papers were often neglected, proving the old adage, "out of sight, out of mind." Archivists who have assisted local officials in the older states do not easily forget their first discovery of a cache of these bundled records in courthouse attics and basements—an experience filled both with revulsion and excitement. Not infrequently, these masses of folded papers constitute treasure troves for historians, worthy of the time and patience required in the delicate process of transferring the papers to proper workspace where they can be humidified and flattened.

Just after the Civil War, a revolution of sorts affected records offices throughout the country. The revolution was in the form of a simple wooden "file box" measuring about four inches wide, ten inches high, and a foot deep—just about the size of a standard sheet of paper folded twice or thrice, wrapped with a ribbon or placed in a paper jacket, and placed upright in the box. Available either singly or as drawers in cabinets of varying sizes, the "file box," with an adjustable rear clamping board holding the documents upright, became almost universally known as the "Woodruff File," named for Edmund W. Woodruff who, with George C. Green, patented the "Paper-File" in 1868 and subsequently sold them by the hundreds of thousands to public officers, from the federal government down to the smallest county and town governments. Fayette County, Pennsylvania, for instance, was an early satisfied customer.

The steps to the first "standard" filing box were described in a United States Senate report in the 1880s:

> Prior to 1865 the files of settled accounts were arranged in bundles of convenient sizes and secured by cord. In 1865 leather straps were substituted for cord at considerable cost. Both the cord and the strap systems were open to serious objections. The unloosing and refastening of the bundles occupied too much time. When carelessly refastened the bundles fell apart and the next time they were handled, the lower part of the papers, being in contact with the shelves, soon became abraded by being pulled out and pushed back. To overcome these objections file boxes were procured, and all the money accounts . . . from 1817 to the present date are neatly and securely filed.[5]

The popular Woodruff File provided something less than an ideal solution to the problem of preserving loose papers. Its invention coincided with the advent of paper mass-produced from wood pulp. Because of the acidic composition of both the wooden files and the wood-pulp paper, coupled with the widespread use of coal heaters and gas burners producing sulphur dioxide in public offices, a heavy toll of deterioration was exacted upon the documents. Furthermore, the

5. U.S., Congress, Senate, 50th Cong., 1st sess., 1888, S. Rept. 507, pt. 2, pp. 254–255.

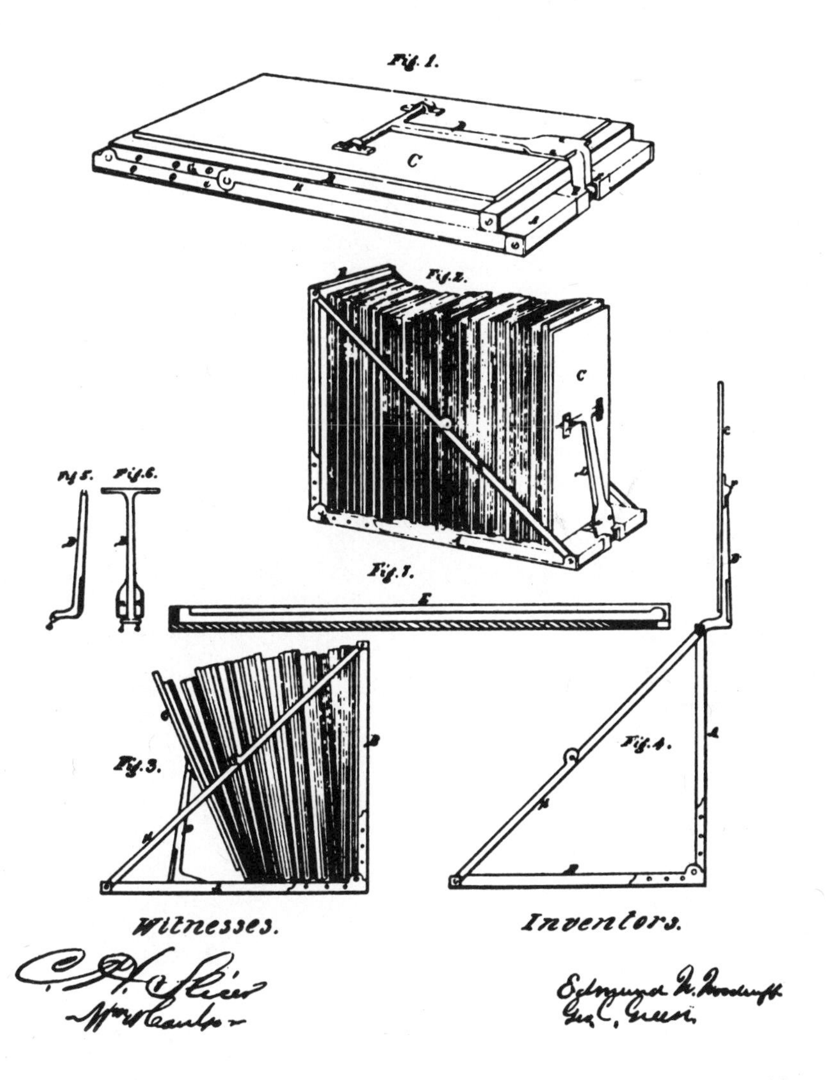

Fig. 3. The Woodruff "Paper-File" after the Civil War provided improved but by no means perfect protection for loose papers. (*American Archivist* 19 [October 1956]: 307)

Fig. 4. Metal adaptations of Woodruff file drawers have continued to be used in public offices, often in harmony with roller-type shelving as shown here in the lower vault of the Baker County Courthouse, Oregon. The steam pipes above the files pose a threat to the records. (Oregon State Archives)

paper at the folds was strained and abraded by the sliding of the drawers. Even the substitution of metal files of similar design and dimensions failed to correct the latter tendency. Still, for half a century the Woodruff File and its imitators were familiar furnishings in county and municipal offices across the land, and even today they may be seen in many local offices.

The next step in improved record-keeping was the flat or vertical file, experimented with since the Civil War but made popular by its display at the World's Columbian Exposition in Chicago in 1893. Perfected by Dr. Nathaniel S. Rosenau, the vertical file allowed original documents up to legal size to be filed without folding. File folders and tab guides increased accessibility. Within a decade or so, reasonably stable carbon paper was invented, and the Taft Commission on Economy and Efficiency in 1912 recommended that federal agencies take full advantage of the newer developments in record-making and record-keeping by substituting typewriter and carbon paper for bound-book registers and replacing folded-document filing with flat filing.

Press-copying and carbon paper were only the first of a series of means of making duplicate copies. The mimeograph, hectograph, and Photostat, by the middle of the twentieth century, began to yield to instant office copiers, some of which, too quickly adopted, produced disastrous results: impermanent copies. Only in the last decade have most manufacturers come to accept their responsibility of promoting only scientifically proven products for recording uses. State archival agencies are in a position to advise local officials concerning the longevity of various types of instant copiers. The author, as a state archivist in the 1960s, tested several instant copiers that were being advertised as producing "permanent" copies. When the tests proved conclusively that the copies were unsatisfactory for use in recording legal documents, the manufacturers were asked for their definition of the word *permanent*. Only one provided a specific answer: ten years!

Microfilm, experimented with in the nineteenth century, became a practical means of providing security and reference copies by the 1930s. By mid-century it was being used as a current recording device through which enlarged paper copies could be made for incorporation into bound books. Shortly afterward, some officials began the exclusive use of microfilm for recording purposes; deeds, for instance, were photographed onto microfilm, and reel or unitized or jacketed microfilm became the official recorded copy. More recently, electronic data systems have been installed in some offices for a variety of recording purposes.

These substitutes for paper records are of very recent origin, and with few exceptions they do not yet pose serious storage problems in the courthouses and municipal buildings of the country. As these latter problems arise, however, their solutions will require the application of expertise beyond that normally found in archivists. While limiting its emphasis to traditional paper records, this book nevertheless presupposes that, once the problem of accumulated records has been brought under control, county and municipal records officers should bring together the talents of information specialists, systems analysts, and archivists to prevent somewhat analagous problems from arising in relation to the more modern machine-readable records.

Early Efforts to Protect Public Records

State assistance in arresting the deteriorating conditions of local records was first extended in the northeast, late in the nineteenth century. Massachusetts in 1884 appointed an inspector to report on the records of the parishes, towns, and counties, and this position evolved into that of a commissioner of public records who, in compliance with later legislation, required the use of specified ink and paper, the storage of records in fire-proof facilities, the repair of worn records, and the surrender of records by a retiring officer to a legal successor. Periodic inspections and fines for violations led to remarkable improvements in the condition of local records and in "bringing the records into prominence, and making them of the importance with which they ought to be regarded."[6] In Connecticut a commission established in 1889 reported on town, probate district, and church records, and a dozen years later a position of public records examiner was established. The Maine legislature in 1897 ordered towns and cities to provide safes or vaults for their records. And, following a fire which destroyed many records housed in the State Library in Albany, the state of New York in 1913 established the office of supervisor of public records for the purpose of enforcing state requirements for local record-keeping.[7]

6. Henry E. Woods, *The Massachusetts Laws and Commission of Public Records* (Boston: Commission of Public Records, 1910).

7. Ernst Posner, *American State Archives* (Chicago: University of Chicago Press, 1964), pp. 68, 131, 147, 194; Kenneth L. Brock, "New York State's Public Records," *National Genealogical Society Quarterly* 64 (June 1976): 115.

These and other early state actions for the safeguarding of local public records resulted mainly from the agitation of historians interested in the records as sources for research; and some states, particularly in the South, put less stress upon proper care of the records in the courthouses and town halls than in their transfer to newly established state archives. Thus the concern was less for administrative needs of the custodians than for the protection of the sources for research. That narrow view was not limited to legislation relating to local records, for the historical profession also successfully lobbied for the establishment of state archival agencies early in the twentieth century and eventually persuaded Congress to establish the National Archives in the 1930s. Initially, these were but repositories for permanent records, and they offered no effective help in the orderly management of records in the offices of origin.

The interests of historians were stimulated and to a degree coordinated by the work of the Public Archives Commission, formed in the American Historical Association in 1899. During its life, the commission published survey reports on local records and called attention to the often deplorable conditions under which they were kept. Finally, in 1932, under the chairmanship of Albert Ray Newsome, the commission published its landmark booklet, *The Preservation of Local Archives: A Guide for Public Officials.*[8] "Official and unofficial surveys," the guide declared, "leave no room to doubt that, with the exception of some of the older states of the Northeast which have applied a science of archive [*sic*] economy, local archives in the United States have not received merited care and are not safeguarded by effective public regulations and practices." Most states, the committee asserted, had neither programs nor laws designed to assure adequate management of local records.

After recounting the ignominious fate that had befallen many valuable records of local governments across the nation, the commission observed: "Fundamental to the proper care and preservation of local records is an appreciative understanding of their importance, particularly by those who have them in custody. Local archives are valuable, first, as business or administrative records; and second, as historical records."

That was a significant statement from a group of historians, for it recognized that public records are not created for historical purposes;

8. Washington: Public Archives Commission, American Historical Association, 1932.

they are, instead, created in the course of and as a by-product of a public officer's performance of his duties. Their primary value, therefore, is as evidence of the proper performance of duties, including the protection of any rights and privileges that might be affected by the documentation. For instance, several types of documents are filed or recorded in connection with the settlement of an estate not so that future researchers can trace family lines or determine property holdings of ancestors but rather to provide legal evidence that the executor or administrator has properly carried out his obligations and has satisfactorily accounted to the court and justified his release from his bond. Thus the records are created to satisfy legal requirements in the settlement of the estate and to provide protection for three parties—the heirs, in their inheritance; the executor or administrator, in faithful performance of duties; and the clerk, in enforcing the statutory requirements for documentation.

The Birth of "Records Management"

Recognition by historians of the importance of records as administrative and legal tools preceded by several years the conduct of the Historical Records Survey, the establishment of the National Archives, and the formation of the Society of American Archivists.

The Historical Records Survey, an activity of the Works Progress Administration, provided employment for some 3,000 persons in a variety of work relating to research materials. Undoubtedly the most valuable undertaking was the survey of county records throughout the nation. Field work was completed in 90 percent of the counties, and 628 volumes of inventories were issued by 1942. Ernst Posner, dean of American archivists, evaluated the results this way:

> From the vantage point of archival administration, the importance of local records and the necessity of caring for them had been brought down to the grass roots, and many improvements had been made. State archival agencies had been provided with inventories of county records that to this day furnish the basis from which measures directed at their preservation must start. Yet perhaps one of the most significant results of the Historical Records Survey was the role it played as a training ground for future state archivists and state archives personnel.[9]

Posner observed, however, that while the survey revealed the great value of local government archives, it did not solve the question of how

9. Posner, *American State Archives,* p. 29.

Probate Court - Proceedings (123-125)

Proceedings

123. PROBATE COURT RECORD, 1848-53, 1855--. 20 vols. (1, 3-17, 17, 18, two unlbld.). Title varies: Probate and Prefect Record Combined, 1848-53; Probate Record, 1855-62; Probate Court, 1863-73; Libro de Prosedimentos de la Corte de Pruebas, Condado de San Miguel, 1873-78; Diario de la C. de P., 1878-83. 1925-28, 1933, 1937 also in Deed Record (and Miscellaneous Record), entry 23.
Minutes of proceedings of probate court including settlement of estates, adoption of minors, appraisal of property, orders of court approving probate of wills, petitions for appointment of administrators, and guardians, and accounting of administrators and guardianship, showing term of court, title of case, case number, name of parties concerned and their attorneys, summary of proceedings, action of court, date, and signature of judge. Includes all activities of county government up to 1876. Arr. numer. by case number. 1848-63, no index; for index 1863-93, see entry 125; 1893-1903, no index; for index 1903--, see entries 127 and 129. 1848-1910, hdw. in English and Spanish; 1910-17, hdw. and typed in English and Spanish; 1917--, mostly typed in English. 222-640 pp. 12 x 7 x 1 to 13 x 12 x 3. 5 vols., 1848-53, 1855-84, H.S.N.M.; 9 vols., 1888-1916, bsmt. va.; 6 vols., 1885-88, 1917--, co. clk. va.

For inventory and appraisement record, 1865-86, 1890-1910, see entry 131; for administrators accounting 1883-87, see entry 136; for subsequent record of county government, see entry 1.

124. PROBATE COURT FILES, 1882--. 156 f. b. (92 lbld. by letters of the alphabet; 53 by incl. case numbers; 11 unlbld.).
Original papers filed in probate cases including wills, letters testamentary, appraisals of estates, letters of administration, oaths and bonds of administrators, letters of guardianship, and decrees. 1882-1908, arr. alph. by name of estate; 1909--, arr. numer. by case number, and chron. thereunder by date of filing. For index, 1882-93, see entry 125; 1893-1903, no index; for 1903--, see entries 127 and 129. Hdw. and typed, some on pr. fms. 4 1/2 x 4 x 9 to 10 1/2 x 4 1/2 x 13 1/2. 117 f. b., 1882-1908, 1939, co. clk. va.; 39 f. b., 1908-38, 1940--, co. clk. off.

125. INDEX TO PROBATE COURT, 1863-93. 1 vol. (1-6 incl.).
Index 1863-93 to Probate Court Record, entry 123, and Probate Court Files, entry 124, showing term of court, names of parties to action, title of estate for guardianship concerned and book and page where recorded. Served as docket during this period. Arr. alph. by name of estate or minor. No index. Hdw. on pr. fms. 308 pp. 17 x 12 1/2 x 1 1/2. Co. clk. bsmt. va.
For docket, 1903--, see entries 127 and 129.

Fig. 5. Nearly 700 volumes of local records inventories were completed by the Historical Records Survey by 1942. This page from the inventory for San Miguel County, New Mexico, is an example. (*Inventory of the County Archives of San Miguel County,* New Mexico [Albuquerque: New Mexico Historical Records Survey, 1941], p. 129)

Fig. 6. The Historical Records Survey often prompted local governments to provide improved housing for their records. Here, Custodian Hubert Barker exhibits the records of the Cleveland (Ohio) Department of Public Utilities in 1936. (Ohio Historical Society)

to preserve them.[10] It did, however, kindle interest in the records, and many counties made conscientious efforts to provide improved facilities for and care of their records. The massive inventories, though usually produced only in mimeographed form, provided administrative offices and research institutions with handy descriptive guides to the rich assortment of records housed in the various courthouses.

The National Archives, which became the chief training ground for the multiplying breed called archivists, was faced with a backlog of nearly two centuries of the nation's records. That staggering accumulation of paper required evaluation (or *appraisal,* in archival language) to segregate and preserve those of value while disposing in an orderly

10. Posner, *American State Archives,* p. 336. See also David L. Smiley, "The W.P.A. Historical Records Survey," in *In Support of Clio: Essays in Memory of Herbert A. Kellar,* edited by William B. Hesseltine and Donald R. McNeil (Madison: State Historical Society of Wisconsin, 1958), pp. 3–28. Records of cities, towns, and villages were also inventoried in some states.

way of those with no further value. In its complex task, the staff of the National Archives could not fail to observe that the proliferation of federal records during the New Deal portended increased problems in the future. Even before America's entry into World War II, the archivist of the United States wrote:

> A prerequisite to the judicious selection of records either for permanent preservation or for disposal is an appraisal of their value, and this appraisal can be made more readily and with greater assurance if the records have been arranged and administered with their permanent preservation or their disposal in mind. Arrangement usually takes place, however, when the documents are filed, that is, when they are first consciously considered as record material. From this chain of circumstance it becomes apparent that The National Archives must inevitably be concerned with the creation, arrangement, and administration as well as with the appraisal, disposal, and preservation of Government records, and that in order to perform its functions satisfactorily it must have a knowledge of the records that can come only from a continuous survey of them.[11]

Problems associated with the war supported the archivist's views. The rapid increase in the number and size of war-related agencies in Washington resulted in pressure for the transfer of additional records to the National Archives in order to make space available for offices; it also resulted in a need for better management of the increasing volumes of records being accumulated in the agencies. Because the National Archives was the main source for personnel experienced in records problems, agencies such as the Navy Department, War Department, War Production Board, Board of Economic Warfare, and the War Relocation Authority enticed away archivists who proceeded to develop in these agencies experimental programs of "records administration"—the precursor of modern records management. One of these was Emmett J. Leahy, who established the Navy Department's records management program, later organized the National Records Management Council, and was acclaimed by his colleagues "for pioneering and winning the acceptance of modern records management among members of the American business community."[12]

11. *Seventh Annual Report of the Archivist of the United States, 1940–41* (Washington: National Archives, 1941), p. 1.

12. Emmett J. Leahy and Christopher A. Cameron, *Modern Records Management: A Basic Guide to Records Control, Filing, and Information Retrieval* (New York: McGraw-Hill, 1965), p. vii. For a fuller tracing of the development of records management in the federal government, see H. G. Jones, *The Records of a Nation: Their Management, Preservation, and Use* (New York: Atheneum, 1969), pp. 24–65; and Donald R. McCoy, *The National Archives: America's Ministry of Documents, 1934–1968* (Chapel Hill: University of North Carolina Press, 1978), *passim*.

Following the war, Congress established the Commission on the Organization of the Executive Branch of the Government, commonly called the Hoover Commission, which selected Leahy to head a task force on federal records problems. The resulting "Leahy Report" influenced the conversion of the archival agency into the National Archives and Records Service which expanded greatly its activities in the area of current records control. Thus the embryonic idea of "records administration"—largely the preparation of disposition schedules—evolved into a new specialty called records management, or paperwork management. Soon afterward, the term *records manager,* meaning a person specializing in records creation and maintenance, began to be used with increasing frequency. Archivists, who had formed a professional association only a dozen or so years earlier, divided over whether to broaden their concern and expertise to incorporate the "birth-to-death" chain of records or to limit themselves to the preservation of the permanently valuable records. Predictably, debates became commonplace between archivists and records managers—debates over whether the records manager was an archivist with additional training in office procedures and paperwork management, whether the archivist was a records manager competent to administer both current and historical records, or whether the records manager was an entirely new breed associated more with administrative management than with concern over the preservation of historical records.

Slow Progress at State and Local Levels

Progress in records management on the federal level was not matched on the state level, though some states did take tenuous steps toward carrying out the recommendations of the Public Archives Commission's *Guide*. A public records act, written by the chairman of the Public Archives Commission, was passed in 1935 in North Carolina, defining official records, specifying the responsibilities of local officials in the making and keeping of their records, and empowering the state's Historical Commission to monitor the condition of the records and to assist public officials in the solution of the problems of filing, preserving, and making available the records in their custody. While North Carolina took steps to enter the field of records management on the state level—opening a "records center" in an old fairgrounds building during the war, establishing a central microfilm service in 1951, and two years later occupying the first specially constructed state records center—it was not until 1959 that a comprehensive local records program was funded by the General Assembly. Georgia began providing limited records services to county governments in 1951, Maryland followed in 1953, and several other states soon sought to offer advisory if not substantive assistance to local officials.

Some municipal governments could not wait for state assistance. New York City, for instance, opened a Municipal Archives and Records Center in 1941 and seven years later required each department to appoint a records officer to administer a records management program. By 1960 the city was housing more than 100,000 cubic feet of records in its center and 20,000 cubic feet in its archives.[13] By the 1950s, Philadelphia, San Francisco, Baltimore,[14] and several other major cities and a few counties had embarked upon records management programs. More recently, in some local governments, sophisticated management systems have revolutionized the management of information with the virtual elimination of traditional paper records. The effect of these systems upon the future availability of data for research has not been fully explored.

Many of the advances that have been made in the past half century in the making, keeping, and using of the records of the nation, the states, and the political subdivisions are attributable to meetings, publications, studies, and training courses provided by professional organizations such as the Society of American Archivists, the American Records Management Association, and the Association of Records Executors and Administrators (the latter two organizations having recently merged to form the Association of Records Managers and Administrators).

Still, a great majority of the political subdivisions in the United States—counties, towns, cities, special-purpose districts, etc.—remain without a program of their own and receive little effective assistance from professionals at a higher level of government. Busy local officials, harassed by the daily problems of an increasingly stifling bureaucracy, the insatiable demands of special interests, and the growing complexities of decision-making, seldom are able to spare the time and thought required for a mature evaluation of their record-keeping pro-

13. James Katsaros, "Managing the Records of the World's Greatest City," *American Archivist* 23 (April 1960): 175–183. New York City has since established a Department of Records and Information Service.

14. An interesting account of the Baltimore story, including a citation to articles on other municipal records programs, is found in Richard J. Cox, "The Plight of American Municipal Archives: Baltimore, 1729–1979," *American Archivist* 42 (July 1979): 281–292.

cedures. A result is an ever-increasing quantity of records with their attendant problems, including a voracious demand for more space and personnel. No one has been so bold as to figure the per capita cost of record-keeping on the local level, but the now-defunct Federal Paperwork Commission in 1977 estimated that the annual cost of federal paperwork alone amounted to about $500 for every man, woman, and child in the United States.[15]

The cost of records is not limited to money. An equally undesirable result of poor record-keeping is the difficulty of information retrieval for current administrative purposes, for public dissemination, and for research. Historians have a particular obligation to encourage the development of economical and efficient records management systems at all levels of government, for, without improved systems, the loss of important research data from the past will pale in comparison with the losses in the future. The proliferation of records in the postwar era is in itself a serious threat to the orderly preservation of records essential to the needs of research.

This book seeks to illustrate the mutual interests of researchers and local public officials and the corresponding need for a better understanding between them. Both make significant contributions to the common weal. Public officers receive, create, and maintain documentation reflective of and essential to the performance of their individual and collective duties. These records serve a function—often several functions—in the on-going conduct of the people's business. They are public property, but they also provide the most lasting evidence of the faithful performance of one's duties. As such, they should be viewed with pride by a public official. Neither a lengthy obituary in the newspaper nor a portrait in a courthouse or municipal building is likely to memorialize a public officer more appropriately than evidence that he maintained good records—evidence that will be clear to future researchers who inspect the documentation carefully preserved through an efficient management system that allows the orderly disposal of records that have served their purposes and the orderly preservation of those with continuing value.

The day is over for the nineteenth-century antiquarian who assumed that public servants held office for the convenience of the researcher, saving every scrap of paper and producing it upon demand. Modern historians must recognize that records are tools of government, intended initially for administrative or legal purposes, and that

15. "Paper Chase," *Time* 112 (July 2, 1978), p. 26.

the enormous increase in the volume of records at all levels of government demands new solutions to old problems. Such a recognition in no way diminishes the importance of that relatively small proportion of records which should be identified as permanently valuable and set aside for preservation and use in appropriate facilities managed by competent professionals. It does, however, increase the responsibility of historians to provide understanding and encouragement to public officials who conscientiously perform their duties by assuring that adequate and appropriate records are created, maintained, used, appraised, and disposed of or preserved in accordance with provisions of the laws and the legitimate interests of the citizenry.

A Word about the Following Chapters

The following chapters are not intended to constitute a detailed handbook for public officials. Instead, they seek to discuss briefly and in lay terms some of the general principles of records management. They are advocative, because wise records management demonstrably produces public benefits—in terms of economy, efficiency, and the preservation of essential documentation. Records management can be neglected only at the peril of the taxpayers. By suggesting various approaches to the development of records management programs, my purpose is to stimulate public officials to examine their current method of coping with their records problems and to evaluate the benefits that may be derived from a well-planned program incorporating a variety of controls such as inventories, retention/disposition schedules, microfilming, and intermediate storage areas. Footnote citations will lead to sources that go into greater detail than is feasible in a book of this length, and an appendix summarizes the extent of professional advice and assistance available from appropriate state agencies. The local official is not alone with his problems; there are others who may be of assistance.

Records management is a development of the past four decades, and like any new specialty, it has not yet achieved a standard vocabulary—despite worthy efforts toward the end. A term means different things to different archivists and records managers around the country. Even the titles of agencies and officials differ from state to state, and the attempt to use the various titles would only add tedium and space; consequently, in the following chapters, the terms *state archives* and *state archival agency* include the records management agency in the few states using the latter title; and *state archivist* means, in a few instances, the state records administrator. The proper names of these agencies in each state are given in the appendix.

The organization of local government and the nomenclature of offices also differ from state to state. For purposes of simplicity, I have used *county* to include parishes of Louisiana and *municipality* (or the adjective *municipal*) to refer to all other political subdivisions—cities, towns, boroughs, villages, special-purpose districts, etc.

2

Establishing a Local Records Management Program

Public Records: Public Property

SAMUEL JOHNSON in the eighteenth century defined a record simply as an "authentick memorial." To record, he wrote, was to register something "so that its memory may not be lost."[1]

Two centuries later, simplicity is no longer in vogue, and the word *records,* modified only by the adjective *public,* now carries this lengthy definition:

PUBLIC RECORDS: All documents, papers, letters, maps, books, photographs, films, sound recordings, magnetic or other tapes, electronic data processing records, or other documentary material, regardless of physical form or characteristics, made or received pursuant to law or ordinance or in connection with the transaction of official business by any agency or officer of government.

Public records are public property, owned by the people in the same sense that the citizens own their courthouse or town hall, sidewalks and streets, funds in the treasury. They are held in trust for the citizens by custodians—usually the heads of the agencies in which the records have been accumulated, but sometimes by other officers to whom custody has been officially transferred by the governing authority. Public records may not be sold, given away, destroyed, or alienated from custody except through an official act of the governing authority in accordance with provisions of any state law relating to their care and disposition.

As public property, public records may no more be altered, defaced,

1. Samuel Johnson, *A Dictionary of the English Language . . .*, 2 vols. (Philadelphia: James Maxwell, 1819), II, p. 3p7.

mutilated, or removed from custody than public funds may be embezzled or misappropriated. Indeed, because records document the conduct of the public's business—including the protection of rights, privileges, and property of individual citizens—they constitute a species of public property of a higher value than buildings, equipment, and even money, all of which usually can be replaced by the simple resort to additional taxes. *It is the unique value and irreplaceable nature of records that give them a sanctity uncharacteristic of other kinds of property and that account for the emergence of common-law principles governing their protection.*

The principles ought to be translated into written law. Counties and municipalities are creatures of the state (a status confirmed by the Supreme Court's one person-one vote ruling), and every state should have a basic records act applicable to all public records, including those of local governments. While all but a few states have laws requiring state-level approval for the destruction of local records, many have not yet adopted comprehensive public records acts spelling out the responsibilities of public officials and providing for state-level standards and assistance (see Appendix A).

A state public records act should, at minimum, contain the following provisions:

1. Formal definition of *public records.* This definition should be inclusive; it should encompass all public records regardless of whether they are exempted from public access (see 5 below).

2. Definition of *custodian* and a description of duties. A custodian is the steward of the people whose responsibilities for protection of the records should be spelled out, including instructions for the use of durable materials and fireproof vaults, requirement for a continuing monitoring of the condition of the records, and authorization for removal of records for repair or rebinding.

3. Regulation of disposition of public records, prohibiting the destruction, sale, alienation, or other disposition of records except upon resolution of the governing body concurred in by the state archival agency, and requiring a custodian to turn records over to a successor.

4. Authorization for the use of the writ of replevin (i.e., the demand by a custodian for the return of a public record unlawfully out of custody).

5. Public access—including examination and copying—and the procedures for exemption of certain records from this provision. It is from this "open-records" section alone that highly sensitive records may be exempted by state law or local ordinance, and any record exempt from this section should be answerable to all other sections of

the public records act. Too often, busy legislators seek to classify records as confidential by declaring them not to be "public records"; such an ill-conceived action in effect denies that the records are owned by the state or locality, thus removing them from the protection of the remainder of the public records act. State and local "Freedom of Information" acts should supplement, not substitute for, this provision in the public records act.

6. Designation and authority of the state archival agency. Even if the agency has been established under a different statute, its responsibility in relation to public records should be summarized in the public records act, where it will be regularly noticed by busy custodians and governing bodies who otherwise may make the grievous mistake of permitting destruction or alienation of public records in violation of state law.

7. Authorization for the use of photographic copies and machine-readable records and the procedures therefor.

8. Establishment of penalty for violation of any provision of the act.

Additional sections relating to the management and security of records may be advisable. Chapter 119, *Florida Statutes,* provides a model for study by states contemplating adoption of a public records act.

The comprehensive state law governing public records of all levels of government should be supplemented by local ordinances in conformity with it but tailored to local needs. The adoption of such an ordinance has the effect of personalizing the state statute and calling attention to its applicability to all local agencies.

The best-written statutes, however, offer little assurance that their objectives will be attained. Indeed, even strong state leadership cannot alone solve the records problems of the nation's counties and municipalities, for local initiative is essential. If that initiative is vigorous enough, an effective records management program can be established and administered even without the encouragement of a state-level agency. The absence of state action is no justification for inertia in the county seats and municipal buildings of the country.

The Need for a Program

More than thirty years ago Margaret Norton, archivist of Illinois, wrote:

> In the days when all documents were written by hand, records were not made unless they were important. It was, therefore, both necessary and

possible to preserve them. Today typewriters, carbon paper, the mimeograph, cheap printed forms, and governmental questionnaires, together with an increasing complexity of governmental functions undreamed of a generation ago, are piling up files in astronomical proportions.[2]

Now, only a third of a century later, public officials are confronted by vastly greater quantities of records than Archivist Norton described during her tenure as one of the leaders of the young profession. The intervening years have brought a growth in the bureaucracy and the introduction of sophisticated equipment and techniques that turn out instant paper copies, machine-readable records, and a wide variety of other informational mediums undreamed of in 1945. No longer is a records management program justified only on the archival grounds of assuring the preservation of records for research use; better management of records is now a necessity if public officials are to be able to handle their mass and variety of records for the benefit of the citizenry. Thus the interests of archivists are merged with the requirements of good administration to demand the establishment at all levels of government of an effective program of records management to eliminate the creation of unnecessary records; to provide for economy and efficiency in the creation, maintenance, and use of those that are necessary; and to devise an orderly system for the preservation of important records and the disposal of those that have served their usefulness.

The objectives of a public records management program, wrote Theodore R. Schellenberg, an archival theoretician, are "to make the records serve the purposes for which they were created as cheaply and effectively as possible, and to make a proper disposition of them after they have served those purposes." He continued,

Records are efficiently managed if they can be found quickly and without fuss or bother when they are needed, if they are kept at a minimum charge for space and maintenance while they are needed for current business, and if none are kept longer than they are needed for such business unless they have a continuing value for purposes of research or for other purposes. The objectives of efficient records management can be achieved only if attention is paid to the handling of records from the time they are created until the time when they are released to an archival institution or disposed of.[3]

2. Margaret C. Norton, "Record Making," *Illinois Libraries* 27 (February 1945): 127. This and other Norton articles are reprinted in *Norton on Archives: The Writings of Margaret Cross Norton on Archival and Records Management,* edited by Thornton W. Mitchell (Carbondale: Southern Illinois University Press, 1975).

3. T. R. Schellenberg, *Modern Archives: Principles and Techniques* (Chicago: University of Chicago Press, 1956), p. 37. Schellenberg served as Assistant Archivist of the United States.

The "father" of records management, Emmett J. Leahy, described the objective more succinctly: "The purpose of records management can be stated in simple terms: *fewer and better records.*"[4]

Schellenberg, Leahy, and other archivists and records managers recognized that the paperwork explosion of recent decades could be brought under control only by the development and implementation of an effective program designed to reduce the quantity of records already in existence, assure the creation of proportionately fewer and better records in the future, and permit the more efficient management of those that are created. As described earlier, the National Archives and Records Service, in which both Schellenberg and Leahy served ably, took the lead in records management in the period following World War II, and some states and a few counties and municipalities followed. Only among the large corporations, however, has the concept of records management been rather generally accepted beyond the federal government, and the few textbooks on the subject have been written chiefly for the business community.[5] These and other professional materials are, nevertheless, useful to public officials in planning a records management program, for the basic objectives are virtually identical in business and government. A few states have published county or municipal records manuals which are essentially guides to the preparation of retention/disposition schedules but which sometimes also provide helpful guidelines for improved records creation

4. Emmett J. Leahy and Christopher A. Cameron, *Modern Records Management: A Basic Guide to Records Control, Filing, and Information Retrieval* (New York: McGraw-Hill Book Company, 1965), p. 17.

5. Among such books, in addition to Leahy and Cameron, *Modern Records Management,* previously cited, are William Benedon, *Records Management* (Los Angeles: Trident Bookstore, UCLA, 1973); August H. Blegen, *Records Management Step-by-step* (Stamford, Conn.: Office Publications, 1965); Wilmer O. Maedke, Mary F. Robek, and Gerald F. Brown, *Information and Records Management* (Beverly Hills: Glencoe Press, 1974). A description of the records management program in the National Archives and Records Service is given in Donald R. McCoy, *The National Archives: America's Ministry of Documents, 1934–1968* (Chapel Hill: University of North Carolina Press, 1978), and H. G. Jones, *The Records of a Nation: Their Management, Preservation, and Use* (New York: Atheneum, 1969). Among the few national publications applicable to local records inventory and appraisal are Philip C. Brooks, *Public Records Management* (Chicago: Public Administration Service, 1961), and *Municipal Records Management and Control* [Management Information Service Report 114] (Chicago [now Washington]: International City Management Association, 1953). Although the latest *Records Management Handbook: Disposition of Federal Records* (GPO Stock Number 022-001-00073-6) is focused on federal records, it will be useful to local officials developing a records program. It may be purchased for nine dollars from the Superintendent of Documents, USGPO, Washington, D.C. 20402.

and maintenance activities.[6] In addition, a few local governments have issued their own publications on records management.[7]

The truth is, however, that there is no single pattern that a county or municipality may copy as its own records management plan. Every program is tailored to local needs, resources, and personnel.

The First Steps

Necessity is said to be the mother of invention, but most local records management programs originate in the minds of dedicated public officials who observe the need for improvements within their own jurisdiction and who become aware of the existence of successful records programs in other jurisdictions. Their introduction to records management may be through the state archival agency, articles in periodicals, speeches and conversations at meetings of county or municipal associations, or visits to other courthouses or municipal buildings. The source of the interest matters little, provided the inspiration is translated into action.

6. Apparently the first printed local records manuals issued by a state were *The County Records Manual* and *The Municipal Records Manual,* edited by H. G. Jones and A. M. Patterson (Raleigh: North Carolina Department of Archives and History, 1960 and 1961, respectively), both of which have since been expanded and brought up to date under the editorships of A. M. Patterson and Frank D. Gatton. One of the best recent manuals is the *Ohio County Records Manual* (Columbus: Ohio Historical Society, 1977). Other useful publications include *Municipal Records Management Program* (Juneau: Alaska Municipal League, 1976); *Records Retention Schedules for Local Governments,* edited by Rockwell H. Potter, Jr. (Hartford: Connecticut State Library, 1978); *Missouri Municipal Records Manual* (Jefferson City: Missouri Records Management and Archives Service, 1973); *County Records Manual,* edited by Joseph F. Halpin (Santa Fe: New Mexico State Records Center and Archives, 1973); *A Guide to Managing Municipal Records* (Albany: New York State Archives, 1977); Craig Blaine, David Larson, and Gerald Newborg, *Local Government Records Manual* (Columbus: Ohio Historical Society, 1976?); *Records Management Manual: Records Disposition,* revised edition (Annapolis: Maryland Hall of Records Commission, 1978); Maurice Lazarus, *A Report on Records of the Minnesota District and County Courts* (St. Paul: Minnesota Historical Society, 1978); *Texas County Records Manual* (Austin: Texas State Library and Archives, 1978); *Retention and Disposition Schedule for Records of Pennsylvania Municipalities* and *Retention and Disposition Schedule of County Records* (Harrisburg: Pennsylvania Historical and Museum Commission, 1973 and 1978, respectively); *Records Retention Schedule* (Salt Lake City: Utah State Archives and Records Service, 1978); and *Local Government Records Workshop Handbook* (Olympia: Washington Division of Archives and Records Management, 1977).

7. For example, *Records Management Manual* (Long Beach, California: Office of City Clerk, 1977?), and *Management Planning Report 2: County Records Management* (Portland, Oregon: Multnomah County Office of County Management, 1977). Several journal articles on local programs are cited elsewhere in this book.

Individual local officials, particularly county and municipal clerks who generally are the major record-producing officers at the local level, have in some instances developed and carried on effective records management programs within their own departments. By preparing and implementing retention/disposition schedules, improving office procedures, and retiring inactive records to less expensive but safe space, a single official can set an example for others in the courthouse or municipal building through the demonstration of substantial benefits. Even more desirable, however, is a program that applies to all departments, and in the remainder of this chapter a broad, centralized program will be advocated. Nevertheless, in a county or municipality where leadership or funds are not available for a centralized program, a single office need not be inhibited from following similar procedures in developing its own program.

A prerequisite for a successful records management program is commitment from the seat of power. A program need not involve a large investment of funds, but it will certainly require a considerable amount of reallocated time and attention. The administrative head and the governing body of the county or municipality must be convinced that the public will benefit from the allocation of the required resources. This commitment can best be obtained through the presentation of a convincing case for records management.

Who makes the case? Anyone—especially an officer whose department is hampered by outmoded facilities and too many records. Or anyone else who recognizes that improvements in records management can contribute to more efficient government. The point is that *someone* must take the lead. One who assumes that lead may find the following steps useful.

1. Make contact with the state archival agency (see Appendix A for name and address) and inquire of possible assistance. In states with a staffed local records program, this assistance will probably begin with an observation visit from a member of the staff. During that visit, the extent of further assistance from the state agency can be determined. Some states provide a staff member to train and supervise local government employees in the conduct of a records inventory and the preparation of retention/disposition schedules; some provide literature such as a local records manual; and all can recommend pertinent literature. A few states also provide the services of a trained records manager to make recommendations on matters relating to the creation and maintenance of current records. Even from the states with no identifiable local records program the county or municipal official can expect

information concerning the procedure for obtaining state-level approval of disposition requests. The *very first step* in the consideration of establishing a records management program should be contact with the state archivist. If he cannot help, he will recommend someone who can. For instance, he can suggest a visit to the nearest Federal Records Center, administered by the National Archives and Records Service; to a neighboring state with a comprehensive local records program; or to another local government that has established a records management program.

2. From the citations in this book, obtain and read one or more textbooks and special manuals. While none of these will be directly applicable to specific local needs, the principles enunciated and the problems discussed will be similar enough to be helpful in visualizing an effective local records management program. Out-of-print items may be borrowed through interlibrary loan. Watch, also, for articles in current journals published by associations of county and municipal officials. Periodicals such as *The County Recorder,* published by the National Association of County Recorders and Clerks, carry reports of local programs across the nation.

3. From references in this book and from information furnished by the state archival agency, contact and—if possible—visit other counties or municipalities that are successfully operating records management programs. Ask for copies of reports and manuals, but remember that reports tend to be self-laudatory and often exaggerate the extent and effectiveness of a program. Personal observation is the best test of the quality of a program.

Only if the three steps suggested above fail to provide satisfactory information should a local official call in a for-hire consultant during the exploratory stage. This is not to suggest that an outside expert cannot be of help; rather, it is to point out that the local official should make a conscientious effort to identify the problems and possible ways of correcting them with government resources before contracting for outside expertise. It may very well occur that the state archivist is not staffed to provide needed assistance and may, in fact, initially recommend such a consultant. Even so, it would be prudent for the local official to become familiar with the literature and experiences of colleagues around the country before bringing in a private consultant—if for no other reason than to be prepared to understand the language and implications of proposals. In case of demonstrated need for a consultant, recommendations should be sought from the state archivist, satisfied colleagues, or the appropriate professional organizations whose addresses are given in Appendix B.

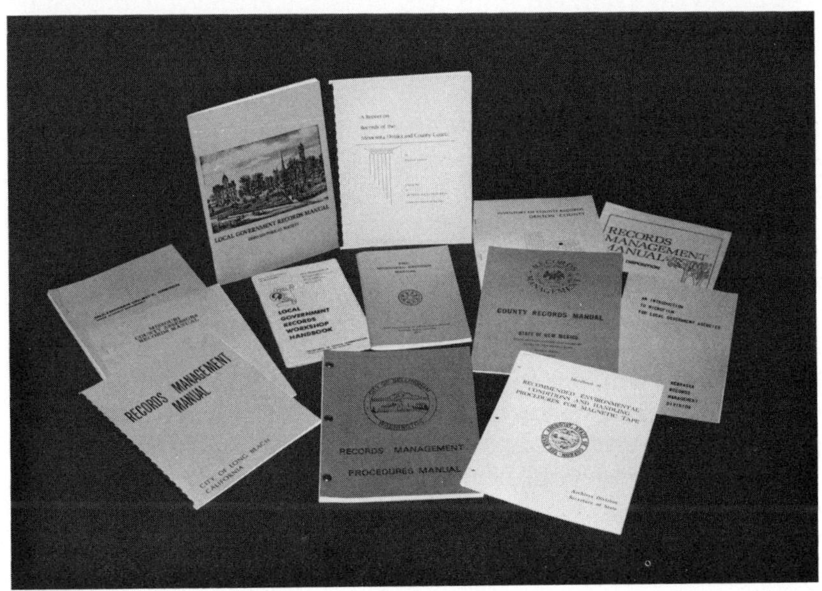

Fig. 7 and Fig. 8. Shown here in Figure 7 are examples of the literature that should form every records officer's bookshelf. Also useful are manuals and guides shown in Figure 8, published by state and local governments. (Courtesy Jerry W. Cotten, North Carolina Collection)

A fifth source of assistance should be the last called upon, for equipment and systems salesmen obviously carry with them a conflict of interest: Their primary duty is to sell their own products. A representative of a microfilm products manufacturer, for instance, can be expected to emphasize the advantages of microfilm, whereas a representative of a paper manufacturer can be expected to stress the importance of paper records. This is not a reflection upon the character of salesmen but, rather, a practical recognition of the role of financial interest in studies and recommendations. Once an objective analysis has been produced, showing the needs of the local government, then professional consultants and representatives of commercial firms may be invited to propose means for assisting in meeting those needs.

The Person in Charge

The extent of assistance provided by the state archival agency will help determine the procedure to be adopted in developing a records management program. As has been pointed out previously, some states can provide the services of a professional staff member to supervise the inventorying and scheduling phases, and a few can even assist in the more technical areas of establishing a records center and instituting improved record-making and record-keeping systems. In these instances, the representative of the state archival agency will, upon agreement with the local government, roughly outline a program, then conduct training sessions for department heads and their chief records personnel. If the state representative can remain on the scene long enough, he may, with authority delegated by the chief administrator or governing body, serve as director throughout the project, utilizing the services of departmental personnel in the inventory and appraisal phases. In such a happy circumstance, the county or municipality will be sharing in the benefits of an archival and records management program that every state should provide.

If, on the other hand, only minimal assistance, or none at all, is provided by the state, the local government has the choice of placing an existing officer in charge of the program, or of establishing a new position of records officer and hiring a specialist. In fairly small counties or municipalities, a conscientious official willing to study existing programs and available literature, can, if given the time, authority, and departmental assistance, satisfactorily perform the assignment. In large, old counties and municipalities whose records problems have grown to substantial portions, a realistic conclusion is that a successful records management program will require the continuing service of a professionally trained records officer. No matter how successfully a records management program is established, it must be continued if the problems are not to recur. In these cases, one or more new permanent positions can be justified, even in the face of tightened budgets, for an objective of good records management is economy, and a successful program can document its savings over a period of time. Certainly an allocation of a fraction of 1 percent of a county or municipality's total operating budget will be wisely spent on records management.

Placement of responsibility for records management will be determined by the nature of governmental organization. A professional records officer's proper place is as near as possible to the officer or group exercising the greatest authority over all departments. In small or medium-sized governments, the records officer should generally report directly to the mayor, manager, other executive head, or to the city council or county commission. In larger governments, the records officer may be placed in the department responsible for the administration of systems and procedures for all departments. The point is that the records officer must have the backing and authority of top management in order to achieve compliance from all agencies of the local government. In addition to a prominent place on the organization chart, the officer needs certain special authority, including the power to disapprove the purchase of records equipment and materials and the allocation of space for records—powers that, if judiciously exercised, will gradually achieve conformity with records policies throughout the departments.

In instances where an outside consultant is engaged to conduct the inventory, draft the schedules, and establish current records policies, the contract should require the preparation of a records management manual and the training of staff members to assure future implementation. After all, conducting a successful records management program is not like periodically taking a harsh purgative; it is more like maintaining a regular, healthy diet.

Introducing the Program

Government employees, accustomed to a plethora of administrative directives commanding compliance, tend—understandably—to hold to familiar routines. Yet, to be effective, a records management program must change the perception of personnel toward "their" records and win the support of all departments. The proposed program must be "sold" on the bases of benefits from compliance and penalties for noncompliance. The task of salesmanship will be easiest if the designated records officer is respected for his knowledge of government, abilities in administrative matters, competence in records management, and skills in public relations.

The program, in addition, requires the designation of a records co-ordinator in each department who can adapt the over-all objectives of the program to the particular needs of specific offices. In small departments, this co-ordinator will probably be the officer in charge; but in larger departments, the position will more likely fall to the person directly in charge of the records operations.

The first influential document issued in connection with the records management program will be the ordinance or policy directive announcing its establishment. That document should be a well-reasoned, well-written narrative explaining why the program is necessary, what it proposes to accomplish, how it is to be administered, and what is expected of employees during its implementation. It should seek compliance through reason, but it should also, in no uncertain terms, cite the means of requiring compliance (for instance, through the records officer's authority to deny requests for additional records equipment or space). In short, the ordinance or policy directive should clearly convey the full commitment of the chief administrative officer and governing body to a continuing program of efficient and economical management of the records of the county or municipality. Diplomacy, of course, will be required throughout the ordinance, and special language may be necessary in relating the program to offices run by independently elected officials, as well as departments carrying on activities funded largely by state or federal monies.

More particularly, the ordinance should specify the authority of the records officer to (*a*) train, assist, and supervise departmental records co-ordinators in the inventorying of all records in the respective offices, (*b*) co-ordinate the appraisal of records for the establishment of retention/disposition schedules, (*c*) study the feasibility of an intermediate storage area, and if found practicable, to establish and administer a records center, (*d*) investigate current records practices and conditions and to formulate improved policies and procedures, and (*e*) review all requests for additional records systems, equipment, supplies, and space. Duties of the departmental records co-ordinators also ought to be specified: to work under the supervision of the records officer in the implementation of the program and to interpret the decisions of the records officer to other personnel within the department. To a large degree, the success of the over-all program will depend upon the good will and conscientiousness of the departmental records co-ordinators whose role in the program should be one of importance and status.

By its nature, the tone of the ordinance or policy directive may be impersonal. Its objectives can be personalized, however, through an early *orientation session* at which the records officer demonstrates competence, attitude, and sensitivity that win the respect of the employees. First impressions are not easily erased, and the ultimate success of the program may depend upon the rapport established at this first general session, during which employees "size up" the records officer. In addition to emphasizing the procedures and benefits of the program, the records officer should show that the final results will be attributable to teamwork in which each staff member plays a role and shares in the benefits and credit. The session should provide ample time for free and open discussion, including questions from skeptics. The experienced records officer will avoid exaggerated claims of potential benefits, for skepticism can undermine the program from the outset.

The orientation session, designed to introduce the program to the entire staff of the county or municipality, should be followed by a *training session* for departmental records co-ordinators and any other employees selected to participate in specific activities such as inventorying. The training session, conducted by the records officer and/or a representative of the state archival agency, goes beyond an explanation of the need, rationale, and objectives of the program. Indeed, it becomes a "how-to-do-it" session. Procedures are described, basic definitions are given, and the role of the departmental records co-ordinators is discussed.

Particularly to be emphasized in the training session is the inventory (see below, p. 41 ff.), in the preparation of which the departmental records co-ordinators play a key role. It is upon the inventory that further decisions and activities are based; consequently, its accuracy and completeness are of critical importance. Two subjects need special attention in connection with the inventory:

1. Both the records officer and the department records co-ordinator must become familiar with the history, organization, and functions of the particular department, for it is only through understanding the agency that the purposes and nature of the records themselves can be understood.

2. The main entries in the inventory (and subsequently the records

retention/disposition schedule) are records *series,* a term that must be fully understood if the entries are to be reliable and useful. A records series has been described as "File units or documents arranged in accordance with a filing system or maintained as a unit because they relate to a particular subject or function, result from the same activity, have a particular form, or because of some other relationship arising out of their creation, receipt, or use." A shorter definition is "a group of records filed as a unit, used as a unit, and which may be transferred and disposed of as a unit."[8] Records co-ordinators should be trained to think in terms of records series, a concept essential to the inventorying process as well as to the implementation of retention/disposition schedules.

Other general principles of records management may effectively be introduced during the training session, but subjects relating to advanced records management, particularly in relation to the creation of records, might well be postponed for consideration at future sessions, after the problems of the backlog have been alleviated.

Publicity through in-house organs can be effective in stimulating a positive attitude toward a records management program. An employee newsletter, for instance, can appropriately carry the names and qualifications of departmental records co-ordinators and reports of their individual and departmental achievements as the program advances. The public news media, too, can promote interest both within and without the government, particularly through "before-and-after" photographs

8. Frank B. Evans, Donald F. Harrison, and Edwin A. Thompson, compilers, "A Basic Glossary for Archivists, Manuscript Curators, and Records Managers," *American Archivist* 37 (July 1974): 430; and *Local Records Workshop Handbook* (Olympia: Washington Division of Archives and Records Management, 1977), p. 18. A more comprehensive definition from the *Oregon Administrative Rules,* Chapter 166, Division 5 (1978), is: ". . . records accumulated over a period of time and arranged in an organized file or set of files which can be described, handled, and disposed of as a unit. A record series may consist of records of a single type or format, or of records kept together because they relate to a particular subject or result from one activity. The physical form of records in a series may vary; paper, film, or other media (including computer storage); volumes, folders, reels, etc., being used at different times. The filing arrangement may be chronologic, alphabetic, numeric, coded, or any combination of filing arrangements. A series may, at a particular time, consist of a single folder, or of hundreds of feet of files. Each record series must be specifically defined and include only records with the same retention period." Finally, David B. Gracy II, in his *Archives & Manuscripts: Arrangement & Description* (Chicago: Society of American Archivists, 1977), pp. 7–8, defines the series as "file units or documents arranged in accordance with a filing system or maintained as a unit because they relate to a particular subject or function, result from the same activity, have a particular form, or because of some other relationship arising out of their creation, receipt, or use."

and stories of reclaimed filing cabinets or improved conditions of records. Great care, however, must be taken to prevent the impression that records—particularly the older ones venerated by local historians—have been or will be cavalierly disposed of. On the other hand, statistics attesting monetary savings provide good news to the public and create greater enthusiasm on the part of county or municipal officials—particularly those who are popularly elected.

An almost universal measurement of the merits of a local records management program is its acceptance throughout the county or municipal government as "our" program, and the effective records officer will seek to inculcate in all departments a pride in their role in a conscious effort to make government more efficient. When representatives of the county or municipal government begin to speak approvingly of "our" records management program at state and national meetings, the program will have acquired a status indicative of its success.

The Inventory Worksheet

Although a cursory survey of the quality, condition, and location of records presumably will have been conducted even before the need for a records management program was established, a far more exact and detailed inventory of all records of the county or municipality is the first major undertaking in the implementation of the program. A records inventory is more than a simple stock-taking or listing; it is a careful exercise during which every records series is measured, labeled, and described on a worksheet to permit a retrospective study of the nature and value of the series in a more physically relaxing atmosphere than that which prevails during the tiresome and tedious work of conducting the inventory. Completeness and accuracy of data, therefore, are essential if the inventory is to serve its purpose, for the inventory worksheets will provide the information on which higher-level personnel, at both local and state levels, will determine the fate of the records. Thus no matter how well the conductors of the inventory know the records, their work will be inadequate unless they transfer a summary of that knowledge to the worksheets. The inventory process should be undertaken with a seriousness of purpose that recognizes a completed worksheet as the most important single document prepared during the entire records management program, for the decisions based upon it will dictate the character of the subsequent phases of the program.

A well-designed worksheet with clear instructions is a valuable aid in the inventory process. As mentioned earlier, inventorying is often a time-consuming, tiring activity, and a good form is needed to provide the shortest and easiest means of recording information. Spaces requiring only a check mark, a number, or a few words can expedite the inventorying and enable the conductors more carefully to write detailed explanations in the larger spaces provided. There are, of course, virtually as many forms as there are archivists and records managers (forms design being a favorite pastime), and a records officer should be encouraged to design a worksheet that best suits local needs. For anyone who prefers simply to adopt an existing form, there is reproduced, facing page 38, something of a composite of worksheets used by the state archival agencies in Ohio, Oregon, and North Carolina. Unlike those forms, however, the worksheet presented here is designed to serve both for inventory *and* appraisal phases and as a rough *and* a smooth (or final) worksheet. The inventory portion of the worksheet is penciled in by the records officer and departmental records co-ordinator. The handwritten worksheets are later brought together and studied by these two officials who will, in the light of additional information gained in the entire inventory process and from the study of any statutory provision affecting the series, confirm or make changes in the initially recommended retention period. When agreement has been reached between the records officer and departmental records co-ordinator (and department head, if he is not the records co-ordinator), the information on the rough, handwritten (and probably pretty well marked-up) original worksheet can be typed onto a clean worksheet. The typed form then becomes more than an inventory sheet; it is both the inventory and the appraisal document that is forwarded progressively to the officials whose approval is required in the formal establishment of a retention period. The advantages of such a dual form are obvious: from the penciled worksheet, a typist can simply type the information onto an identical form; the records officer and others familiar with the worksheet can more easily proofread the typewritten copy; and higher-level reviewers will be impressed by the neatness and clarity of the edited, typed copy and thus be spared the pain of trying to read scrawly, dirty, original worksheets.

For each records series, the following information (keyed by number to spaces on the worksheet facing page 38) will be needed:

1. Department, division, and subdivision. This information places the records in their organizational setting. Many local departments will

have no divisional breakdown, but larger ones may—for example, Clerk of Court (department), Criminal Court Division, Records Section.

2. Name and title of officer immediately responsible for the records—i.e., the person best informed about their contents, purpose, and value.

3. Records series title. For a discussion of "records series," see above, page 36. The series title should be as specific and descriptive as possible. Generally, it will be the same as that assigned by the department having custody of the records, but if the currently used title is misleading, the records officer should discuss with the department the possibility of adopting a more accurate title. Vague terms, such as "Reports," "Requisitions," and "Correspondence," should be avoided; instead, the title should reflect the specific kinds of reports, requisitions, and correspondence.

4. Records series number, if needed, may be added later in arranging the series for listing in the retention/disposition schedule.

5. Description of the records—content, purpose, function, how and by whom created and used, and other pertinent data to help determine the value and lifespan of the records. Form numbers, if any, should especially be noted.

6. Inclusive dates. If most of the records cover a shorter period than the inclusive dates, that information should be noted. If the series consists of undatable records (e.g., personnel folders), descriptive words such as *active* or *inactive* may be substituted.

7. Are the records still being created?

8. If so, list the estimated annual accumulation in cubic feet.

9. How are the records arranged within the series? (e.g., alphabetically by name, chronologically by date of entry into service, numerically by registry number, etc.).

10. Statistics on how often and for how long the records are used. This information is important in the appraisal process and should be obtained from the person accustomed to servicing the records.

11. If there are other copies (including microfilm) of the series, where are they located and which should be considered the "record" copy? For instance, policy directives presumably go to each department, but the "record" copy usually is the one kept by the issuing office.

12. Relationship of the series to other records series (such as indexes and summaries). For instance, one records series may be indexed

by or may serve as an index to another group of records; or vouchers may be listed also in a voucher register.

13. Exact location of the series—building, office, location on floor plan. Give as precisely as possible. Fill out a worksheet for each separately filed or shelved portion of the series.

14. Space occupied by the series, in cubic feet. Conversion tables may be found in standard records management textbooks. For instance, one letter-sized file drawer holds about 1.5 cubic feet; a legal-sized drawer, about 2.0 cubic feet. Bound volumes should be counted both in number of books and in cubic feet.

15. Size of record—width by height (and in case of bound volumes, thickness).

16. Description and quantity of filing or shelving equipment occupied by the series. Abbreviations or symbols may be used (for example, 1=one letter-sized drawer, 1_4=a letter-sized four-drawer cabinet, L=a legal-size drawer, and L_5=a legal-sized five-drawer cabinet). The purpose of this information is to determine how much equipment and space can be reclaimed if the records are destroyed or moved to another place.

17. If there are state laws or local ordinances governing retention of or access to the series, or if the state archival agency has established a retention period for the series, summarize provisions.

18. Suggested retention period. After inspecting the records and orally discussing their use with personnel most knowledgeable about them, the records officer and departmental records co-ordinator should agree on a *tentative* recommendation for retention. The retention period is entered with the anticipation that it may be altered after further study and consultation during the appraisal phase, but its entry at the time of the inventory, while the nature of the records is fresh in mind, may serve a useful purpose later.

19. Additional comments, especially in regard to interest evidenced in the records by historians, genealogists, attorneys, or other users.

20-21. Signatures of records officer and departmental records co-ordinator, with dates of inventory.

The remaining spaces, 22 through 26, are reserved for the appraisal process.

The inventory worksheet, of course, is simply a convenience. Its usefulness depends upon the care with which it is filled out during the inventorying process, studied during the appraisal process, and kept up to date during a continuing program of records management.

Conducting the Inventory

The records officer assists in and supervises the inventorying in all departments; consequently, the task should proceed in only one department at a time, and all of the records of a particular department should be covered before inventorying is begun in the next one. That allows the records officer to give undivided attention to each office for a period of time, increasing an understanding that will be valuable in the subsequent appraisal process. It is perhaps unimportant which department is selected for first attention, but many archivists prefer to start with the one with the greatest prestige—perhaps the office of the county clerk or recorder or the town or city clerk. Equally as justifiable would be the selection of the department having the most urgent need of relief or the one likely to produce the most dramatic cost-saving results. The author would choose the department exhibiting the best atmosphere of support, expecting that its interest and co-operation would have a salutary and contagious effect upon other departments.

Following the selection of the department, another question arises: whether to begin with the active (or "office") files, or with the seldom-used records in storage. If the procedure suggested above is followed, advantages would be derived from starting with the most recent and active records, because these are the materials that are closest at hand, can be most easily understood, are the best known to the departmental personnel, and will shed light upon the older records. While a case can be made for starting with the stored records, there may be a temptation to begin discarding before the inventory of all of the department's records has been completed. That temptation must be resisted; otherwise, once the pressure for space is removed, the entire program may lose its sense of urgency and wholeness. *Beware of quick "housecleanings."*

Although the inventory is conducted by the records officer and the departmental records co-ordinator, the department head (if he is not serving as records co-ordinator) and files personnel should also be involved. Custodians have a right to be "possessive" of their records, and they may view the inventory process as simply "messing around in our records." Even verbal reassurances may not allay that suspicion; it can best be overcome by a demonstration that the inventorying of records series does not involve the reading of individual documents and gossiping about their contents. The records officer sensitive to the possessiveness of custodians toward their records will seek to minimize that rather natural tendency, for departmental personnel may help determine the location and nature of records. Veteran employees in particular should be asked whether they know of the location of records that have been stored away over the years or which were forgotten during the movement of offices. Attics, basements, unused fireplaces, and tunnels are prime hiding places for older records, and the discovery of a cache of long-forgotten records is not at all unusual during records inventorying. Historian Philip Jordan described town records that "were found only after sidestepping litter in a basement police garage, then passing through the milk inspector's office and a dank, pre-Civil War passageway, and on to an ancient closet." In that damp vault he found scores of record books, tossed about without any semblance of order, but within a week he had traced, in those "forgotten" records, the stories of a cholera epidemic, an errant town marshal, and an ordinance aimed at preventing floating houses of ill fame from docking at the wharf.[9]

The difficulty of the task of inventorying will be dependent upon the adequacy of the worksheet, the quantity of records and how well they have been filed or shelved, and the condition of the storage areas. The more difficult the task, the more likely is the need for improvements in the management of the records within the department. The inventory thus not only yields information about the nature of the records; it also reveals much about the administration and procedures of the department.

Principles of Appraisal

Completion of the inventory of one department's records calls for a decision on whether to pause and conduct an appraisal of those records or to proceed immediately with the inventorying of the records of all other departments and *then* to conduct the appraisal of the records of all departments when the entire inventory process has been finished. The former procedure carries the advantage of freshness of information; it also enables the records officer and departmental records coordinator to continue working together until the retention/disposition schedule is drafted and sent on its way for higher-level approval. On the other hand, duplication of records in more than one department may be detected and the recommended retention periods adjusted appropriately if the appraisal phase is delayed until all departments

9. Philip D. Jordan, "In Search of Local Legal Records," *American Archivist* 33 (October 1970): 380.

have been inventoried. On balance, the appraisal of one department's records immediately after completion of the inventory appears advantageous. Retention periods, after all, can be revised if subsequent information dictates amendments.

The completed inventory worksheets form the raw materials for the evaluation or "appraisal" of each series of records. If the inventory has been conducted carefully and pertinent information entered on the worksheets, the appraisal process will be facilitated greatly; if, on the other hand, the appraisers must frequently reinspect the files for clarification of entries, the process will naturally be prolonged. *The key to good appraisal is a good inventory.*

Appraisal is described as "the process of determining the value and thus the disposition of records based upon their current administrative, legal, and fiscal use; their evidential and informational or research value; their arrangement; and their relationship to other records."[10] The objective of the appraisal process is the determination of how long and under what conditions particular records series ought to be preserved, if not permanently. Appraisal is not biased toward retention *or* disposition; it seeks to assure the preservation of records as long as prudence and good government require, but it also seeks to contribute to good government by legally authorizing disposal when particular records have fulfilled their usefulness.

Archivists describe records as having two types of basic values: *primary* (or administrative or operational) value and *secondary* (or archival, research, or informational) value. Most records are made or accumulated to accomplish actions, to report on or record them, or to pass on information. Whether required by law or simply incidental to the performance of duties, records usually have a sense of immediacy about them; they are seldom made for posterity. Their primary value, therefore, is to the department or office that created or received them and that is legally responsible for them. Some records, however, are important for reasons other than those for which they were originally created or accumulated. Deeds, for instance, are initially recorded to

10. Evans, Harrison, and Thompson, "A Basic Glossary," p. 417. Useful discussions of appraisal standards may be found in Maynard J. Brichford, *Archives & Manuscripts: Appraisal & Accessioning* (Chicago: Society of American Archivists, 1977), and Theodore R. Schellenberg, *The Appraisal of Modern Public Records,* National Archives Bulletin No. 8 (Washington: National Archives and Records Service, 1956). States differ in excluding certain "records" from the legal definition of the word. Nonrecord materials usually include stocks of publications, library or museum materials made or acquired and preserved solely for reference or exhibit, and the like. Definitions established by the state archives should be adhered to.

protect landowners, and wills are recorded to assure the proper settlement of estates. For succeeding generations, however, these records take on secondary values: They may be used for the tracing of land titles and family lines, for finding one's ancestral home, for determining the price of land, and for a variety of other informational purposes.

The terms *primary* and *secondary* are more theoretical than useful; consequently, four more practical measurements of records values have been adopted for use in the appraisal process. The immediate as well as the future usefulness of each records series should be measured against them. Records should be preserved as long as they have one or more of the following values:

1. *Administrative value.* Administrative or operational value refers to the usefulness of records to the creating agency in the conduct of its ongoing activities, though it may also apply to the usefulness of records to another office of the same governmental jurisdiction. As stated earlier, records are normally made or received in connection with the performance of the functions and responsibilities of an office, and they have administrative value as long as they are needed to document the activity to which they are related. Conversely, their administrative value may diminish when the transactions to which they relate have been completed. In addition, however, some records help document the history, organization, functions, policies, and operations of an office and are needed to give consistency and continuity to its actions. Such records "contain precedents for policies, procedures, and the like, and can be used as a guide to public administrators in solving problems of the present that are similar to others dealt with in the past. They contain the proof of each agency's faithful stewardship of the responsibilities delegated to it and the accounting that every public official owes to the people whom he serves."[11] These records are said to have "evidential" value, a characteristic measured in terms of both administrative and research value.

2. *Fiscal value.* A responsible accounting of public funds and property requires the maintenance of adequate documentation at least until

11. Schellenberg, *Modern Archives,* p. 140. The famed English archivist Sir Hilary Jenkinson wrote that an administrator should have his records "in such a state of completeness and order that, supposing himself and his staff to be by some accident obliterated, a successor totally ignorant of the work of the office would be able to take it up and carry it on with the least possible inconvenience and delay, simply on the strength of a study of the Office Files." Hilary Jenkinson, *A Manual of Archive Administration,* 2nd ed., rev. (London: Lund, Humphries, 1965), p. 152. See also Michael Cook, *Archives Administration: A Manual for Intermediate and Small Organizations and for Local Government* (Folkestone, England: William Dawson & Sons, 1977), p. 61.

the accounts are audited; some financial records have additional uses. Records of local activities funded partially by state and federal funds may require retention periods established by those levels of government. Proposed retention periods for fiscal records should be reviewed by the chief fiscal officer of the county or municipality.

3. *Legal value.* Retention periods for certain records may be fixed or influenced by specific statutes or regulatory codes.[12] In addition, however, records may have legal value for individual citizens or the government. Records relating to birth, marriage, property, and suffrage, for instance, help protect individual Americans in their rights and privileges of citizenship; and agreements, contracts, leases, titles, minutes of meetings of administrative and quasi-judicial bodies, and a variety of other records help protect the government itself from adverse legal decisions. Thus, ironically, records affect the citizens in both a positive and a negative way. The county or municipal attorney should review proposed retention periods to assure the adequate retention of records of legal value.

4. *Archival value.* Based solely upon administrative, legal, or fiscal values, relatively few records require permanent preservation. However, many records have continuing value for other purposes. The term *archival value* encompasses two more specialized types of values, evidential and informational. As indicated above, selected records documenting the origin, organization, development, and functions of the creating department constitute the "evidence" needed to understand the purposes and operations of a department. More common, however, are records containing information on persons, places, subjects, events, and transactions—information that usually was not the primary justification for the creation of the records, in the first place. Such records may be important as historical documentation on specific persons, places, subjects, events, and transactions—for instance, the date and place of birth, marriage, land ownership, political affiliation, and death of an individual citizen. This is the stuff of biography. Or the minutes of a town meeting may document in considerable detail the extraordinary measures taken following a disastrous cyclone. More commonly, however, historians and other researchers seek aggregate

12. State laws should usually be searched, along with any schedules established by the state archival agency. For records resulting from federally funded programs, the *Guide to Record Retention Requirements,* published annually in the *Federal Register,* should be consulted. Federal audit is required before federally funded project records may be destroyed. In some states, court records may not be disposed of without the approval of an agency of the judiciary.

information on persons (for example, ethnic origins of the residents of a particular village), places (like the number of brick houses in a town in 1790), subjects (such as the effects of poor roads on rural voting habits), and events (for example, the calendar of events during a centennial observance).

Of the four measurements of records value, that of archival importance is the most difficult to apply. First, its consideration is based upon future needs, not all of which can be foreseen by even the most sagacious archivist; and second, forever is a long time, and the decision to preserve a particular records series permanently carries a perpetual obligation of the citizens to pay the bill for preservation. Thus, while the determination of whether records deserve permanent preservation ideally should be made solely on the potential use of the information contained in them, in fact the implications of that decision must be weighed against the cost. A few records deserve permanent preservation because of their uniqueness or intrinsic value, regardless of their informational content. A bill of sale signed by George Washington, for example, has both a sentimental and monetary value, and no custodian would think of sending it to the incinerator. Similarly, the earliest records of a county or municipality are relatively more important than their counterparts for later years, because they constitute virtually the entire documentation of the formative years. In a county or municipality that had no newspaper or other means of recording activities in its early years, these old records are of proportionately greater value than the same types of records in modern times. It would take a courageous town clerk in New England, for instance, to destroy seventeenth- or early eighteenth-century records of any type. Care must be taken, however, to avoid allowing age to become a dominant factor in determining archival value. The determination of archival value should be made by a professional archivist, though he will seek the opinions of all persons involved in the appraisal. For example, a veteran custodian will have observed from experience which of the older records attract historians, genealogists, and other researchers; and the local historian will contribute valuable insight into historical events and personages likely to be of interest to generations ahead.

The Retention/Disposition Schedule

The establishment of retention periods is a joint undertaking. The administrative or operational value of records can best be gauged by administrative personnel—the makers and keepers of the records—

who know why they were created, who uses them and for what purposes, frequency of reference, and how long they are active. Fiscal value, on the other hand, may best be determined by the auditor, and the legal value by the county or municipal attorney. The archival or research value falls into the expertise of the archivist, through the recommendations of the previously mentioned officers should certainly be considered. Retention periods are best reached through the reconciliation of differing initial opinions, and the appraisal process is best carried out by joint discussions between the custodian (including key files personnel), auditor, county or municipal attorney, records officer, a historian, and a representative of the state archives. In the absence of a staff member from the state archival agency, the reviewers should have in hand the state statutes and any guidelines published by that agency, such as a local records manual, general records retention/disposition schedule for local governments, or special forms required in the disposition of records. In states without such publications, those of neighboring states, counties, or municipalities may be suggestive.

The consultation begins with a study of the inventory sheets, sorted out by organizational pattern and function. All sheets for a records series, wherever portions of it are located, combine to explain the "four w's" of evaluation (what, when, where, why). Time will be saved if an instant copy of each penciled worksheet is furnished to each reviewer, the original being reserved for final notations. That will permit each reviewer to make notes for subsequent study in instances of lack of unanimity at the first meeting. Each reviewer, though primarily interested in perhaps only one of the four "values" against which each series is measured, contributes a different perspective and consequently plays an important role in the evaluative process. That role is more apt to be asserted in an around-the-table consultation than in the hurried reading of the worksheets during a normal, hectic workday. In the review, the records officer is the leader, the negotiator, the secretary, who attempts to reconcile disparate views, for it is the records officer who will translate the recommendations into a workable retention/disposition schedule.

The mechanics of recording appraisal decisions varies from program to program. The city of Long Beach, California, for instance, uses a separate form on which all records of a single title, regardless of location, are listed and evaluated. On the other hand, combination forms, such as the one printed facing page 38, provide space for recommended retention periods and require no additional form for the evaluative process. In using the combined form, the reviewers simply confirm or alter (in pencil) the periods initially suggested by the records officer and departmental records co-ordinator. Upon the completion of the review the records officer then makes necessary changes on the master inventory worksheet and hands it to a clerk who prepares a neatly typed duplicate. The typed worksheet is then signed by the records officer and departmental records co-ordinator and forwarded to the other officers who, successively, may be required by law or ordinance to approve the retention periods. If a higher-level reviewer rejects the suggested retention period, negotiations must be resumed; otherwise, when properly signed, the worksheet provides the legal authorization for the transfer of the entry to a formal records retention/disposition schedule.

Procedures in some states permit the transfer of the proposed retention periods to the retention/disposition schedule prior to their formal approval by higher-level officials. The entire schedule in those instances is then submitted for approval by the required signatories. A mild objection to that more expeditious procedure is the tendency for less information to be transferred to the schedule than was contained on the worksheets—information that might be useful to a conscientious reviewer. On the other hand, where top-level approval tends to be simply a formality, the procedure can save a great deal of time and expense.

Some states also permit "one-time disposal authorizations," particularly for old series no longer being created. Thus, instead of entering these series on the retention/disposition schedule, the records officer forwards the inventory worksheets (or specially designed authorization request forms) and, upon appropriate approval, the records are disposed of and the forms filed as evidence of conformity to the laws or regulations governing disposition. This shortcut also has the advantage of expedition and may increase the drama of the records management program by showing immediate savings in releasing filing equipment and space for reuse.

A rather convincing case, however, can be made for the incorporation of *all* records series into the retention/disposition schedule, and that is the procedure the author recommends. The schedule, if it includes all records belonging to the county or municipality, becomes more than an administrative tool; it takes on the character of a historical document, because it provides a permanent description of the records that existed at the time of the inventory. Even after countless series of records have been disposed of, there will remain for future researchers a descriptive stock-taking of all the records owned by the county or

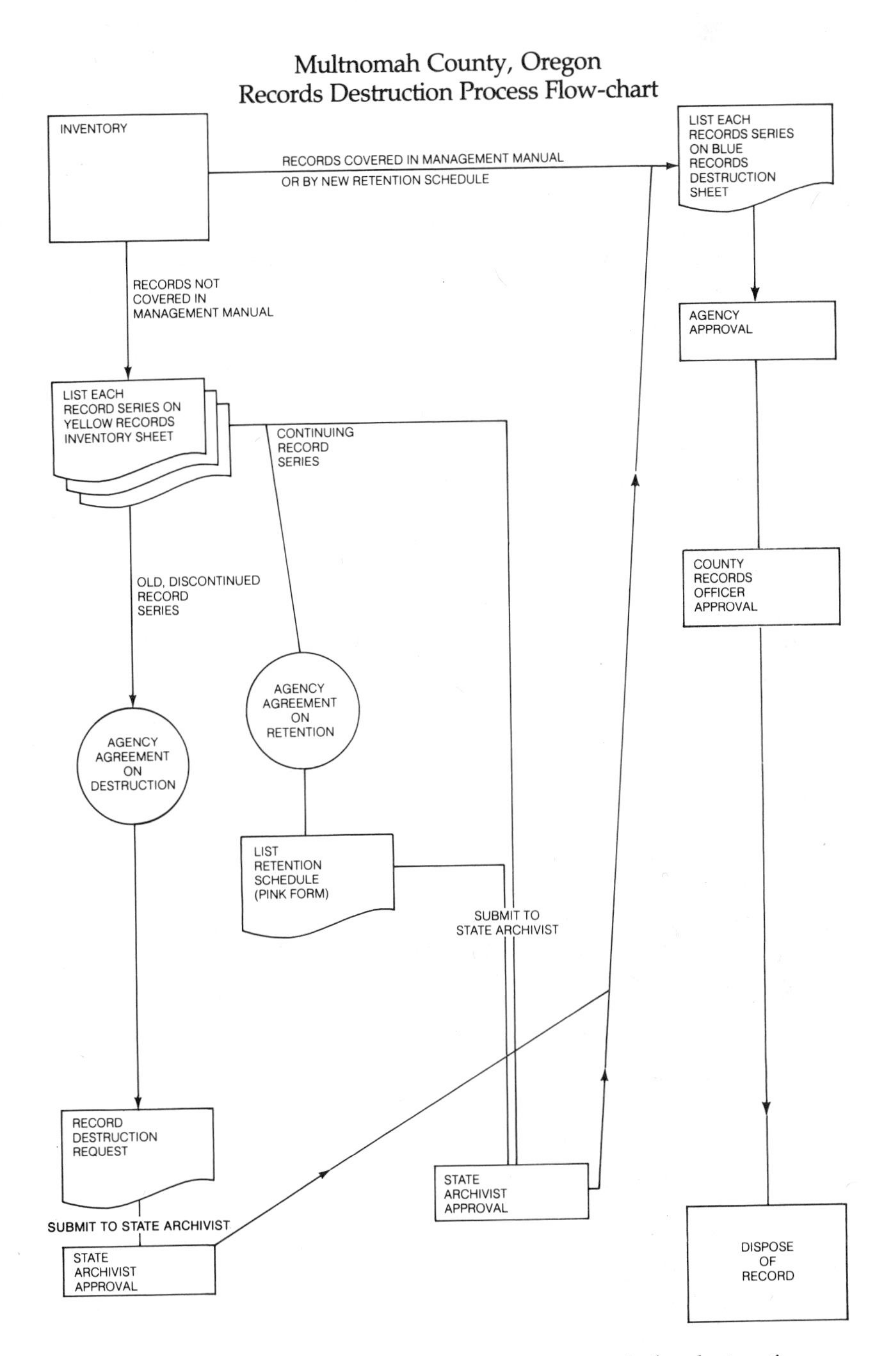

Fig. 10. Procedures for obtaining appropriate approvals for destruction vary from state to state. This flowchart is used by Multnomah County, Oregon. (Courtesy Jerry Royer, Multnomah County Records Officer)

municipality at one particular time. By studying the schedule, a researcher will be able to visualize the way a department functioned, for the inventory of its records, accompanied by the importance attached to them by means of retention periods, will help explain how its functions were carried out.[13] To be sure, the schedule will undergo periodic changes, but a copy of the initial document, set aside for permanent preservation, may become a significant "record" on its own merits.

As in so many aspects of records management, the format for a records retention/disposition schedule depends upon the state and local government concerned. North Carolina, recognizing the inhibitiveness of a printed form, utilizes a typed format that allows expanded data as each series may require. Other states, like Ohio, use a convenient columnar form. Multnomah County, Oregon, has developed its own columnar form. Regardless of the format of the schedule, series should be arranged by department (for example, all records series of the county clerk are listed separately from those of the county auditor), and within each department, the series should further be arranged by operating unit or function (for example, all records relating to the settlement of estates should be grouped together and not scattered among those relating to the recording of deeds). In effect, the schedule should reflect as nearly as possible the organizational pattern of the department and the functions within each operating unit. Such a grouping facilitates an understanding of the relationships of the records and also makes easier reference to the schedule. Each series at minimum should be given a control number, series title, short description (if not clear in the title), and should list quantity, inclusive dates, and retention period. If particular series or segments thereof are to be transferred to an intermediate storage center or archival repository, the retention period should indicate the schedule.

If the worksheets containing proposed retention periods have not received individual approval by the local heirarchy and by the state

13. Records officers can perform a useful service to posterity by maintaining a file containing samples of records destroyed—particularly of discontinued series. This, of course, can get out of hand, but a judicious selection is both practical and desirable. These samples can provide evidence of the types of records created and maintained during the life of an agency, even though they have outlived their usefulness and have been, except for the samples, destroyed. "Sampling" can also preserve documentation of one governmental unit to exemplify the types of records destroyed in other units. For example, a state might schedule for permanent preservation (in the original or on microfilm) the records of the early school lunch program for just one county. Several states require the preservation of local tax records for one year out of each ten. Some archivists require the preservation of samples of all forms. As the volume of paper records increases, the potential advantages of sampling also increases.

archivist, the records retention/disposition schedule must run the gamut of reviews and approvals. Indeed, because the schedule carries continuing authority for records disposition, it requires careful preparation and review. The schedule may, of course, be amended, but retention periods, once established, tend to become sanctified. They should, therefore, be realistic when established. Even if the periods were agreed upon by the custodian, auditor, attorney, and local archivist or historian during the appraisal process, a wise procedure would be to allow each a final review of the retention/disposition schedule. Errors may have been made through misunderstanding or transcription, or additional thought may have affected judgment concerning a particular retention period. The delay occasioned by this final local review will be more than compensated for by the assurance that the document has the support of all public officials whose records are included.

Whatever the format of the schedule and regardless of earlier approvals, the records retention/disposition schedule should be signed by the required officials. The document will probably be several dozen pages in length for a small or medium-sized county or municipality, or several hundred pages for a metropolitan community, and the approvals normally will be attached in the form of a title page. The signatures attest that state law and local policies have been followed in the establishment of the retention periods, that records may be legally disposed of in accordance with the provisions of the schedule, and that any liability that the custodian of the records might incur "shall cease and determine" when he has carried out the provisions of the schedule. This latter certification is an important incentive for the orderly disposition of records that have served their usefulness as indicated in the schedule.

It should not be overlooked that, in nearly every state, records retention/disposition schedules must be signed by the state archivist or otherwise be in conformity with state laws and regulations pertaining to public records. Some states require the additional approval of the state auditor or another state official or commission (such as, in Pennsylvania and Washington, a state-level local records commission). These reviews are designed to safeguard the state's interests as well as those of the county or municipality and the citizens.

Implementation of the Schedule

Upon its approval by the required authorities, the records retention/disposition schedule becomes a legally and administratively approved and enforceable directive for the effective and timely reten-

DAILY COMPLAINT LOGS

Arranged chronologically. Contains daily record of complaints filed with health district showing name and address, date, location, and nature of complaint. Retention: Two years.

DAILY REPORT FORMS - SANITATION

Arranged chronologically. Contains daily activity report of sanitation inspector. Data used in compilation of health services report. Retention: Five years. Administrative.

DAIRY PRODUCERS INSPECTION RECORDS

Arranged alphabetically by dairy producer. Shows location, permit number, date of inspection, violations, and specific recommendations. Retention: Five years. Administrative.

DAIRY PRODUCERS RECORDS

Arranged alphabetically by dairy producer. Contains copies of dairy producer permits and inspection forms showing location, permit number, date of inspection, violations, and specific recommendations. Retention: Five years. Administrative.

DAIRY PRODUCERS SPOT CHECK FORMS

Arranged alphabetically by dairy producer. Shows location, permit number, date of spot check, observations, and specific recommendations. Retention: Current year and one year past.

DEATH CERTIFICATES

Arranged alphabetically by decedent. Contains original certificate of death showing date, place, and cause of death; last residence, age, date of birth, race, and occupation of decedent; funeral home; signature of physician; and date filed. Retention: Permanent. Historical. Administrative. Legal.

DENTAL RECORDS

Arranged alphabetically or numerically by patient. Contains dental work records, patient records, record charts, evaluations, dental examinations, and mouth charts. Retention: One year after treatment.

DRILLERS AND INSTALLERS PERMIT STUBS

Arranged numerically by permit. Contains stub showing name, permit number, date, and amount of fee paid. Retention: Six months after audit. Fiscal.

EPIDEMIOLOGICAL CASE RECORDS (ORC 149.43)

Arranged alphabetically or numerically by patient. Contains examinations, investigations, physician's treatment, diagnosis,

Fig. 11. A page from the retention/disposition schedule for general health district records in Ohio. (*Ohio County Records Manual* [Columbus: Ohio Historical Society, 1977], p. 200)

tion and disposition of all records series contained in it. Like any directive, however, it must be complied with if it is to accomplish its objective of fewer and better records. The objective will not be achieved if the schedule is simply filed away or shelved. The records retention/disposition schedule must become an *action* document. A copy of the entire schedule should be prominently displayed and often referred to in at least the office of the chief executive officer of the county or municipality. Copies of departmental portions of the schedule should be conveniently available in each department, and the records co-ordinator should not only implement the provisions but also familiarize the remainder of the staff with those provisions. No less frequently than annually the departmental section of the schedule should be reviewed. At that time provisions are carried out, but, in addition, a determination is made as to whether changes are desirable in the retention periods and whether new series of records have been created, thus dictating additions to the schedule.

Regardless of its format, the retention/disposition schedule is likely to contain retention periods expressed in a variety of ways:

1. In terms of *immediate action,* especially in the case of a recorded series no longer being created: "Destroy immediately" or "Transfer to Archives immediately." Such action should be taken soon after the retention/disposition has been promulgated.

2. In terms of *action after a period of time:* "Retain 7 years, then destroy." Annual monitoring of the schedule will result in the destruction of one year's increment annually.

3. In terms of *action following a specified event;* "Retain until 2 years after audit, then destroy" or "Retain until 5 years after closing of case, then destroy." These provisions require alertness to determine when the conditional event occurs, for the additional retention period begins at that point.

4. In terms of *action conditioned on other actions by the records officer or coordinator:* "Retain until microfilmed and film has been verified, then destroy originals (or transfer originals to Archives)" or "Retain in chronological order until microfilm has been verified, then merge with 'Deeds Uncalled for, Alphabetical.'" Again, the departmental records co-ordinator will need to be alert to avoid the accumulation of a backlog of actions.

5. In terms of *action involving intermediate storage* (if a records center is provided): "Retain in office 2 years, then transfer to Records Center to be held 8 years, then to be transferred to the Archives."

In addition to these examples, of course, retention periods may

AUGUST 1978

CITY OF PORTLAND
RECORDS CONTROL SCHEDULE

SCHEDULE NUMBER	DESCRIPTION OF RECORDS	RETENTION AND DISPOSITION
5600	METROPOLITAN HUMAN RELATIONS.	
5600-01	AFFIRMATIVE ACTION FILE. Includes clippings, reports etc. on city, county and national affirmative action programs, EEO reports. Arranged chronologically within groupings.	Permanent.
5600-02	METRO HUMAN RELATIONS COMMITTEE REPORTS. Includes committee minutes, activity reports, member appointments, citizen volunteers, clippings, correspondence for the Employment committee, Equal Justice committee, Education committee, Housing committee, Nominating committee and the Awards committee. Arranged alphabetically by committee.	Permanent.
5600-03	PROJECT DISCRIMINATION FILE. Includes complaints against private clubs, welfare, utilities, city, media, housing, police, employment, etc. Arranged by subject of complaint then chronologically. CONFIDENTIAL.	7 years after resolution of case. Bring forward reoccuring cases as needed. Transfer resolved cases 3 years after resolution or as volume warrants.
5600-04	SPECIAL SUBJECTS FILE. Includes reports, correspondence, clippings, proclamations, photos on Indians, hippies, age discrimination, Black history, adult literacy, Jewish/Israel facts, neighborhood facility task force, senior citizens etc. Arranged alphabetically by subject.	Permanent.
5600-05	ORGANIZATIONS FILE. Includes correspondence, reports regarding bureaus, Urban League, American Jewish committee, Albina Neighborhood Improvement, Black Justice Committee etc. Arranged alphabetically by organization.	7 years. Retain in office 3 years then transfer to City Records Center.

Fig. 12. A page from the retention/disposition schedule for records of the Metropolitan Human Relations Commission, Portland, Oregon. (*City of Portland, Oregon, Records Manual* [Portland: Office of City Auditor, 1978], p. 189)

range from simple to highly complex, particularly if permanently valuable local records are accepted for preservation in the state archives or a regional repository administered by the state archival agency. Oftentimes retention periods make direct reference to laws or regulations affecting the records; in those cases the departmental records co-ordinator may need to obtain a legal opinion from the county or municipal attorney.

State and local policy will dictate the steps required to carry out the provisions of the schedule. In some states, a properly approved records retention/disposition schedule authorizes the governing body of a county or municipality to carry out the retention periods contained therein without further reference to the state archival agency. Some states provide similar authority for the disposition of records contained in published general schedules; others still require state-level approval for destruction regardless of the provisions of the retention/disposition schedule. In the latter case, the additional approval appears to be precautionary, giving the state archives one last opportunity to review the proposed disposition and to requisition the records if, in its opinion, they are of archival value.

In an effort to monitor the implementation of records retention/disposition schedules, some states, like Ohio, provide a special certificate for use in reporting on disposition. Such a procedure encourages frequent reference to the schedule and helps make it an action document. In states where no report to the state archives is required, at minimum a record of each destruction action should be made locally. The city of Long Beach, California, for instance, uses a form originating with the records officer and approved by the department head and city attorney, then sent to the city council for approval. The approved records destruction request form is filed as a part of the case history of the records retention/disposition schedule, and the minutes of the city council provide evidence that the destruction of the records was properly authorized.

This recitation of some of the paperwork involved in disposing of records suggests that even records managers have become ensnarled in the "red tape" that helps account for the paperwork explosion that they are called on to solve. It is true that archivists and records managers are not immune to overdocumentation, but no one local government or state archival agency requires as much reporting as has been discussed in this chapter—which has, of necessity, referred to policies of many different states. As has been pointed out repeatedly, the very first step in the consideration of the paperwork problems is familiarization with the laws and regulations of the state in which the county or municipality is located. When the laws and policies of just one state are studied, the obstacles to the establishment of an effective local records program fall easily, particularly with the aid and encouragement of the state archival agency.

3
Coping with Quantity

THE establishment of a records retention/disposition schedule presupposes the application of a variety of solutions to the problems of accumulated records. The extreme decisions are immediate destruction or permanent preservation. Between these extremes are several alternatives, including destruction of records after a period of time or destruction of the originals only after they have been microfilmed. Another alternative may involve the transfer of the records to an intermediate storage area. The alternative chosen will be determined by the reference requirements and the physical characteristics of the records.

A Purgatory for Records

If the two chief adversaries of wise records management are a zealousness to destroy everything and an unwillingness to destroy anything, valuable allies are practical middle grounds that will encourage the preservation of records *only* as long as they serve a justifiable purpose in as efficient and as economical a manner as possible. One of these allies is an intermediate storage area, commonly called a records center.

The concept of a records center was introduced during World War II by the War and Navy departments, popularized by the National Archives and Records Service after the war, and adopted by some corporations and state and local governments in the 1950s. By definition, a records center is a "facility, sometimes especially designed and constructed, for the low-cost and efficient storage of and furnishing of reference service on semicurrent records pending their ultimate disposition."[1] In other words, a purgatory for records.

The costs of keeping records in government offices can be deceptive. First, there is the replacement value of filing equipment: a standard four-drawer metal filing cabinet costs close to $100 and holds about six cubic feet of records. A half-dozen corrugated boxes, each with a capacity of one cubic foot of records, may be purchased for as little as $1.50. The transfer of six cubic feet of records to boxes and the reuse of a cabinet, therefore, may result in a cost avoidance of nearly $100, and that cost avoidance can be repeated each time the cabinet is emptied for reuse. Second, there is the cost of space: a file cabinet requires about six square feet of floor space (two square feet for the cabinet, two square feet for the drawer to open, and two feet for the clerk using the records) which, at a rental value of $8 per year per square foot, costs nearly $50 per year. In a records center with a high-density storage capacity, the space costs perhaps $1 per cubic foot per year, or a space saving of more than $40 per year for the contents of one file cabinet. Third, there is the cost of reference to the records. Many variables make generalizations difficult in regard to personnel costs, but there is ample evidence that prompt, efficient, and less costly reference services can be provided for most records when they are held in a records center. Together, the savings in equipment, space, and personnel are impressive enought to justify an examination of the records center concept by local officials. Normally, records referred to less than two times per file drawer per month are eligible for record center housing.

Happily, a records center offers advantages in addition to economy and improved reference service, for it also can provide for orderly preservation of semiactive records of permanent value. It can also offer a place where a more intensive analysis can be made of "rats' nests" of records not easily identified and appraised during the inventory phase of the records management program. Furthermore, a properly designed and staffed records center may also serve as the archival repository for a county or municipality if a more appropriate archives cannot be provided (see below, p. 77 ff.).

Most of the published literature on records centers relates to the large operations of the National Archives and Records Service and several states and international corporations.[2] A records center, how-

1. Frank B. Evans, Donald F. Harrison, and Edwin A. Thompson, compilers, "A Basic Glossary for Archivists, Manuscript Curators, and Records Managers," *American Archivist* 37 (July 1974): 428.

2. Among the best discussions of records centers are those contained in William

ever, need not be large to be efficient and economical. Indeed, more and more counties and municipalities are making effective use of compact storage areas equipped with high-density shelving. The most successful of these provide space for semiactive records of all departments, though in some instances they serve only one large department, such as that of the county clerk.

Nor does a records center have to be specially built, though the most efficient ones usually are. Warren County, New York, utilizes a portion of the lower floor of a new courthouse; Marion County, Oregon, makes use of the basement of a nearby building; and Westchester County, New York, converted a large one-floor corporate building into a records center.

In evaluating the need for an intermediate records storage area, local officials must first dispel any notion that a records center is simply a place where useless records are dumped. In the first place, such records as really are useless ought to be destroyed; and in the second place, orderliness, compactness, and security form the trinity of records center philosophy. Its prime objective is the elimination of the need for "dumping areas" by providing properly designed, equipped, and staffed space where less active records can be housed and serviced more efficiently and economically than they can be if kept in prime office areas or forgotten storerooms and other hiding places. The records center seeks to bring all records into the light where their usefulness can be monitored.

Generally, only records with a specific retention period should be placed in a records center. In that regard, the center is a sort of waystation; records will either be destroyed after the retention period has passed, or they will be transferred to archival custody. Exceptions to that general rule are made when records need to be observed and studied to determine their value and when records require "weeding" (i.e., the retention of only selected documents from the series). In these instances, however, it is best to hold these materials in a staging area of the center rather than placing them with the scheduled series on the shelves.

Benedon, *Records Management* (Los Angeles: Trident Bookstore, UCLA, 1973); Wilmer O. Maedke, Mary F. Robek, and Gerald F. Brown, *Information and Records Management* (Beverly Hills: Glencoe Press, 1974); Victor Gondos, Jr., *Reader for Archives and Records Center Buildings* (Ann Arbor [now Chicago]: Society of American Archivists, 1970); and A. W. Mabbs with Guy Duboscq, *The Organization of Intermediate Records Storage* (Paris: UNESCO, 1974 [available from UNIPUB, Inc., P.O. Box 433, New York, N.Y. 10016]). Of value also is *Federal Records Center Facility Standards* (Washington: National Archives and Records Service, up-dated periodically).

Physically, a records center can be of just about any size, shape, and arrangement imaginable, so long as it affords economical and efficient housing and prompt service. Certainly small counties or municipalities have no need to build, equip, and staff a model records center, but they may indeed be able to remove from existing space broken-down furniture, outdated equipment, and chaotic mounds of discarded records; the space gained, if secure, properly ventilated, and outfitted with shelving, might provide housing for a significant proportion of the records now crowding front offices. Nor is it always justifiable for medium-sized counties and municipalities to build a new records center, for very often satisfactory if not ideal space can be found in existing buildings, whether government-owned or not. Such converted space is likely to be less efficient in terms of arrangement and capacity, but it often can provide essentially the same services as a more conventional records center.

In contemplating the establishment of a records center in existing space, local officials would do well to review some of the characteristics of specially designed centers as found in published literature already referred to. Some of these features are:

1. *Staffing:* Unless the records center is to be simply a communal storage area with marked-off spaces for each department (in which case it can hardly be called a records center), it should be under the control of a designated official (usually the records officer) and staffed by one or more persons. Only records center personnel should accession, assign space numbers for, and shelve the records, maintain locator files, and furnish reference service. A "do-it-yourself" operation almost inevitably breaks down; on the other hand, records center personnel view the center as an entity to be administered in a tidy, orderly, and efficient manner, making maximum use of space and staff.

2. *Physical characteristics:* A records center should be built of fire-resistant materials, generally above-ground with adequate floor-load capacity, well-lighted, atmospherically controlled, equipped with a sprinkler or alarm system, and provided with a telephone or communication system. Efficient use of space is achieved by means of metal shelving and cardboard cartons. Six cartons 10½ inches high by 12 inches wide by 15 inches deep (each holding one cubic foot of records), accommodating both letter-size and legal-size materials, will conveniently fit on a shelf 42 inches wide and 32 inches deep. Greater economy can be achieved in the case of relatively inactive records by putting units back to back and "double valving" the boxes (i.e., putting one behind another). The higher the shelving, the greater the econ-

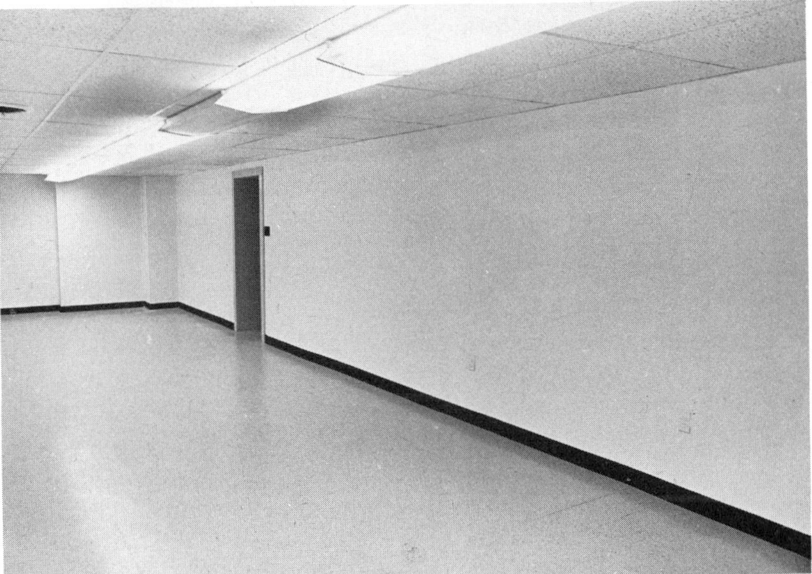

Fig. 13 and Fig. 14. Space occupied by records haphazardly stored, as seen in Figure 13, can be converted to productive use, as shown in Figure 14. (North Carolina Division of Archives and History)

omy; movable ladders with spring wheels enable the practical use of shelving reaching to 14 feet, thus achieving a ratio of as much as five cubic feet of records for each one foot of floor space in the building. In addition to the shelved area, space—preferably partitioned off—may be provided for offices, workrooms, microfilm operations, and shredding. Magnetic tapes, microfilm, and other sensitive materials may require a fire-resistive, separately partitioned area meeting stricter standards.[3] If the records center also is to serve as the archives for the county or municipality, it will be desirable to provide a separate vault-type room for the records classified as archives.

3. *Protection:* In addition to efficiency and economy, a records center must provide a high degree of protection of the records from many dangers—unauthorized entry, theft, vermin, fire, water, excessive or inadequate temperature and humidity, etc. Officials considering a records center should at minimum read the National Fire Protection Association's booklets, *Protection of Records 1975* and *Manual for Fire Protection for Archives and Record Centers 1972*.[4]

4. *Convenience:* Because only records with some degree of value are placed in a records center, adequate provision must be made for prompt reference service. Convenience is served if the center is located near the public offices making use of the space, but distance is mitigated when the records center staff furnishes information from the documents—or the documents themselves—through a regularized procedure. Most needs for information from the records can be furnished by the records center staff by telephone; when documents are needed by the creating office, they can be sent by messenger. Essential to the success of any records center operation is a sense of service on the part of the staff, for the center will thrive only to the extent that the records, or information from them, can be furnished promptly and willingly to the offices to which they belong. After all, only physical custody is transferred to the records center; legal custody remains with the department in which they were created or accumulated. Normally the only exceptions to this rule are records of defunct agencies for

3. The Oregon Archives Division, for example, has issued a *Handbook of Recommended Environmental Conditions and Handling Procedures for Magnetic Tape*. For guidelines on microfilm storage, see P. Z. Adelstein, "Preservation of Microfilm," *Journal of Micrographics* 11 (July-August 1978): 333–337.

4. NFPA No. 232 and 232AM, available from National Fire Protection Association, 470 Atlantic Avenue, Boston, Massachusetts 02210, for $4 each. The first booklet contains, in addition to standards for fire protection, a perceptive chapter on "Management of Records." See also Harold E. Nelson, "Fire Protection for Archives and Records Centers," *Records Management Quarterly* 2 (January 1968): 19–23.

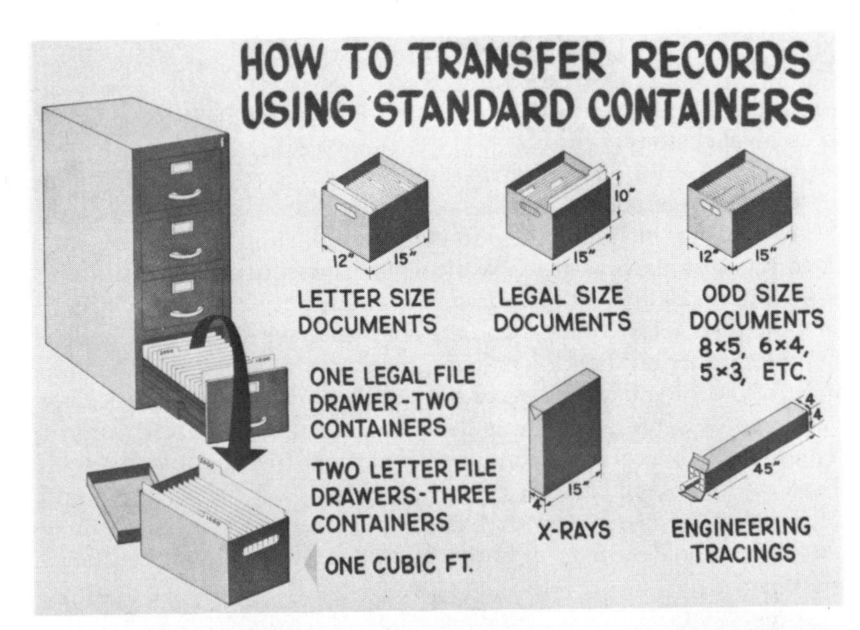

Fig. 15 and Fig. 16. Reusable filing equipment and space can often be freed by the transfer of records to cartons (see Figure 15). (William Benedon, *Records Management* [Los Angeles: Trident Bookstore, UCLA, 1973], p. 69). Compact shelving of cartons in a records center as shown in Figure 16 provides low-cost protection of the records. (North Carolina Division of Archives and History)

which there is no successor agency, and records that have been retired to archival custody.

Records center design has become something of a science among records management specialists who are familiar with trends in record-making, including the imminent introduction of more sophisticated types of machine-readable systems. Consequently, the planning of a new, specially built records center ought not be undertaken until after the responsible officials and the architect have studied the professional literature on the subject. Even so, literature is quickly outdated, and those contemplating a records center would do well to visit their state records center, if there is one, and the nearest federal records center. Though local operations are infinitesimal in size compared with those of the federal centers, personnel of the National Archives and Records Service, the agency that first popularized records centers, may be able to translate their experiences into lessons adaptable to local needs.

In summary, an intermediate storage area, where semiactive records can be more efficiently and economically housed and serviced, is practical for all but very small counties or municipalities. To serve its purpose properly, however, a records center must be operated as an integral part of the local records management program, providing low-cost housing and high-level service. The planning and outfitting of a records center require not only capital expenditures but also a commitment for adequate staffing and an enforcement of its use through the implementation of records retention/disposition schedules.

Microfilm: Panacea or Problem?

Microfilming is a process of photographically producing onto film miniaturized images of paper records.[5] The reduction ratio varies ac-

5. Literature on microfilming is plentiful, though relatively little of it is addressed specifically to local government needs. Exceptions include Robert L. Pugh, "Records Management and Information Retrieval: Developing a Micrographics System for Local Government," *Management Information Service Report* 7 (May 1975), published by International City Management Association, 1140 Connecticut Avenue, N.W., Washington, D.C. 20036; and John T. Donahue, "Getting Local Government into the Twentieth Century Before the Twenty-First Century Arrives," *Journal of Micrographics* 11 (July-August 1978): 356–358. The single most useful survey of microphotographic uses is found in *Microfilm and the Courts: Guide for Court Managers* (Williamsburg, Va.: National Center for State Courts, 1976), which constitutes a summary of the 800-page *Microfilm and the Courts: Reference Manual,* published by the same organization. The National Micrographics Association (8728 Colesville Road, Silver Spring, Maryland 20910), rep-

cording to the size of the documents, the width of the film, and the degree of clarity desired. Although modern equipment, film, and processing allow high reduction ratios, there is some diminution of detail when the reduction is very great. Microfilm images are enlarged to an eye-readable size on a microfilm viewing machine, and paper enlargements of varying sizes may be made on reader-printers or on more sophisticated equipment.

Somewhat like the earlier Woodruff File, microfilm once was oversold as a panacea for records problems. Its indiscriminate use in the 1950s undoubtedly wasted a great deal of the taxpayers' money, for tons of records that ought to have been scheduled for destruction were instead recorded on microfilm.

The abuse of microfilm, however, should not obscure its practicality for a variety of uses today. Invented during the Franco-Prussian War and used extensively in the production of "V-Mail" during World War II, microfilm had by the 1930s become a practical means of duplicating documentary materials. The substitution of safety-base film for the earlier unstable and dangerous nitrate film increased its acceptance in the federal government. Beginning in the 1940s microfilm was introduced to many county officials when the Genealogical Society of the Church of Jesus Christ of Latter-Day Saints, with the approval of state archivists, inaugurated a program of microfilming, in the county courthouses, selected records of genealogical interest. A strange machine, operated by a stranger representing a strange church (Mormonism was then rare in the older states where the filming started) did more than cause gossipy tongues to wag in county seats: perceptive government officials began to see the merits of microfilm beyond the purpose for which the Mormons were filming the records. For instance, they found some comfort in knowing that master microfilm copies of their deeds, wills, estate records, and vital statistics were being stored in a safe place in Utah, and that in the event of the loss of the original records through fire or otherwise, their contents would be preserved on the film. Except in states where county officials were paid from copying fees, officials also welcomed the placement of a reading copy of the film in the state archives. Go to the state capital, they could now tell those pesky genealogists!

---

resenting the industry, publishes a wide assortment of literature on the subject, including the useful *Introduction to Micrographics* and *Operation Practices Manual*. Though written for federal government operations, the National Archives and Records Service's book, *Managing Information Retrieval: Microfilming Records*, can be useful at the local level.

ANNUAL COST OF KEEPING ONE CUBIC FOOT OF RECORDS IN THE INACTIVE RECORDS CENTER

At ______________________________

	Cost	Annual Charges
1. QUARTERS		
a. Rented space—annual rental ______________	—	$
b. Owned space—______________	$	$
2. LIGHT, HEAT, TELEPHONE AND JANITOR SERVICE ______________	—	$
3. SHELVING	$	—
a. Cost of money ______ % of Item 3. ______________	—	$
b. Income tax ______ % of Item 3. ______________	—	$
c. Depreciation-Annuity ______ % of Item 3. ______________	—	$
4. CARTONS (Total cost of cartons)	$	—
a. Cost of cartons divided by ______ years of life. ______________	—	$
b. Cost of money ______ % of ½ of Item 4. ______________	—	$
5. FURNITURE AND FIXTURES (Including desks, chairs, tables, office equipment, ladders, hand trucks, etc.)	$	—
a. Cost of money ______ % of Item 5. ______________	—	$
b. Income tax ______ % of Item 5. ______________	—	$
c. Depreciation-Annuity ______ % of Item 5. ______________	—	$
6. LABOR AND SUPERVISION (Supervisor and ______ emps.)	—	$
a. Social Security, Relief and Pensions, and Group Insurance ______ % of Item 6. ______________	—	$
b. General Supervision ______ % of Item 6. ______________	—	$
7. TRANSFER OF RECORDS TO THE CENTER (Include cost of preparing transmittal forms, and transporting cartons to center.) (This charge is applicable to first year only) $__________/carton x __________ cartons per year. ______________	—	$
8. TOTAL INVESTMENT ______________	$	—
9. TOTAL ANNUAL COST OF OPERATION		
a. First year—Total Items 1 through 7. ______________	—	$
b. Subsequent years—Total Items 1 through 6. ______________	—	$
10. TOTAL VOLUME OF RECORDS STORED ______________ cubic feet ______________	—	—
11. ANNUAL COST OF STORING ONE CUBIC FOOT OF RECORDS		
a. First Year —Item 9a divided by Item 10 ______________	—	$
b. Subsequent years—Item 9b divided by Item 10 ______________	—	$
12. ANNUAL COST OF KEEPING ONE CUBIC FOOT OF RECORDS IN OFFICE FILES ______________	—	$

Date ______________ Prepared by ______________________

Fig. 17. The economy afforded by transferring records to a records center may be estimated by the use of this chart. (Adapted from William Benedon, *Records Management* [Los Angeles: Trident Bookstore, UCLA, 1973], p. 118)

The Mormon copying program had a considerable impact upon the popularization of microfilm, for it gave firsthand evidence to local governments that the new medium could be used to provide a security copy of important records and, by the simple procedure of duplicating the film, simultaneously produce additional reference copies that could be placed in other repositories. Thus the experience of the Mormons, coupled with that of agencies of the federal government and some corporations, confirmed the feasibility and economy of duplicating records for convenient use in other locations. The achievement had enormous implications for researchers throughout the world.

Not lost on those observing the use of microfilm was the lesson of potential space-saving. On the average, two huge deed books containing a thousand pages and weighing perhaps thirty pounds could be recorded on one hundred-foot roll of 35-millimeter microfilm. Surely somewhere a county clerk must have examined two of his deteriorating deed books of the 1880s and wondered if the day might come when one roll of film could be substituted for those almost unhandleable volumes.

Until mid-century, most of the duplication of records for security and reference was done by planetary cameras using 35-millimeter film, but with the improvement of high-speed rotary cameras utilizing 16-millimeter film, the duplication of unbound materials became less costly and more popular. It was at this point that the microfilm industry cranked up its advertising campaign and sold a bill of goods to gullible officers of both government and business. The figures looked good: for only a fraction of a cent, a duplicate requisition could be microfilmed; for only a few dollars, an entire file drawer of requisitions could be filmed, after which the records could be destroyed and the drawer could be reused. That was good reasoning, to a point, but the adoption of a retention period for duplicate requisitions would have enabled the destruction of these papers *without filming*. The cost of this filming, therefore, was wasted money.

Sadly, then, microfilm swept in as a panacea for accumulated records, and many public officials adopted the technological approach of microfilming rather than the intellectual solution of developing a records management program that would incorporate selective microfilming as one of several techniques for attacking their records problems. For that is what a microfilm program should be: *one of several techniques* in a records management program. To be sure, it is an important one that, used wisely, contributes to economy and preservation.

Microfilm most commonly comes in hundred-foot lengths with

widths of 16 and 35 millimeters, wound on reels or in cartridges or cassettes. However, additional formats—all of them "flat"—have been developed for microimages, including *aperture card* (one or more images mounted in a rectangular window cut in a computer card), *film jacket* (strips of film slipped into a series of pockets in a rectangular, transparent jacket), and *microfiche* (a series of images arranged on one sheet of film usually cut from 105-millimeter roll film). Important recent developments, *updatable microfiche* and *ultrafiche,* promise to increase the adaptability of fiche for procedural recording systems. Together the various formats of microfilm are called *microforms,* and the art of microfilming is known as *micrographics.*

The camera film, when developed, is a negative copy—i.e., the tonal qualities are reversed so that a standard document appears with white letters on black background. This master copy has but one purpose: the reproduction of additional microfilm copies as needed. Duplicate copies—film, diazo, or vesicular—normally are positive—i.e., black letters on white background—though direct duplicating film

Fig. 18. The variety of formats of microforms is illustrated by the equipment shown here. (Courtesy National Micrographics Association)

MICROFILMING RECORDS

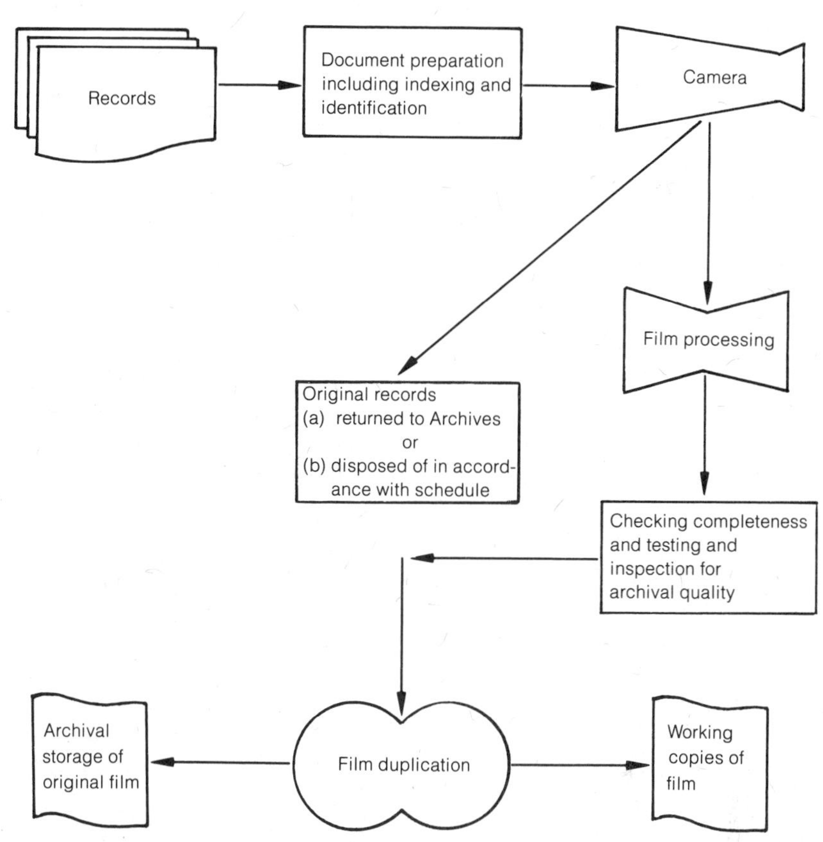

Fig. 19. Steps in the microfilm process shown here include careful identification, indexing, testing and inspection of the film to assure archival quality, and reproduction of working copies. (Adapted from *Managing Information Retrieval: Microfilming Records* [Washington: National Archives and Records Service, 1974], p. 12)

facilitates the production of duplicate negative-reading reference copies when desired. The master negative should never be used as a reference copy lest it be scratched or otherwise damaged by the reading machine, and it should be provided clean, cool, dry, and secure vault storage in accordance with the American National Standards Institute's specifications for microfilm storage.

A microfilm system—particularly an in-house operation—demands a considerable understanding of micrographics and its capabilities and limitations. Merits of microfilm include space-saving, rapid retrieval, file integrity (i.e., documents remain in the order filmed), low cost of duplicate copies, possible labor-saving in retrieval and filing, compatibility with computers, and faithful visual quality. Limiting factors include the relatively high cost of the master negative, preference of the average citizen to see and hold the original document or a paper copy, difficulty of comparing one image with another, high degree of technical knowledge required of the staff producing and using the film, necessity of a variety of equipment for particular uses, and difficulty of updating. The cost of installing an in-house microfilming system is considerable—up to $50,000 for equipment alone in a medium-sized jurisdiction purchasing its own planetary and rotary cameras, processor, inspection equipment, duplicator, readers, reader-printer, film-storage cabinets, and accessories. Supplies—film, cartons, labels, chemicals, etc.—might be figured currently at fourteen dollars per roll. Each duplicate roll costs less. In addition, an in-house operation requires one or more employees with special training in the principles of microphotography to handle the technical aspects of the work. The preparation of materials for filming and the operation of the camera are suitable for any reliable office employee.

The alternative to establishment of an in-house operation is the contracting of all or a portion of the work to a microfilm service company. Although contract work has proved satisfactory for many local governmental units, the very special nature of public records requires that the actual filming be done on government premises under the supervision of the custodian of records. Public records should not be permitted beyond official custody.

In short, a microfilm program is expensive. But so are all other records systems. Economy, convenience, preservation, and public acceptability should provide the test in determining the need for a microfilm program.

More specifically, under proper circumstances microfilm can be justified for the following purposes:

1. *Preservation*—the substitution of a microfilm reading copy and the withdrawal of the original from regular use. This application of microfilm is normally limited to records of great intrinsic value, delicate records that can be handled only with extreme care, and records whose size, shape, or condition make handling difficult.

2. *Research*—the distribution of copies of records on microfilm to

permit their use in archives, libraries, and other research institutions. Microfilming is far cheaper than printing; in addition, microfilm accurately copies the original, showing signatures, alterations, and imperfections—features of importance to researchers.

3. *Security*—the deposit of a microfilm copy of vital records in a vault for retrieval in the event of the catastrophic loss of the records themselves. This security copy should be preserved in the state archives or some other safe, off-premise facility.

4. *Quick reference*—the use of sophisticated indexing systems and cartridge-type microfilm for rapid retrieval. Automatic retrieval systems usually produce a microfilm image in less time than is required to locate the original document—if it has been preserved. A reader-printer enables the production of a paper enlargement within seconds.

5. *File continuity*—safeguarding against misfiling or alteration. Unlike loose papers, images on microfilm cannot get out of order (assuming that they were filmed in proper order).

6. *Economy of space*—the substitution of microfilm for the original documents, which are then destroyed or otherwise disposed of. Microfilm can be stored in perhaps 2 percent of the space required for the original records, but microfilming for reasons of economy is cost-effective only for records that are required to be kept for a long period of time—for example, twenty years. Some records managers claim that they can keep paper records in their records centers for up to forty years at less than the cost of microfilming. Some records, of course, such as large, cumbersome materials that tax normal storage facilities, may be eligible for microfilming for convenience, even though they have a shorter retention period.

7. *A combination* of two or more of the above purposes.

While microfilming can contribute significantly to the solution of some problems of accumulated records and indeed should be promoted in those cases, its greatest potential lies in its adoption as a direct recording medium.

Counties, in particular, provide recording offices for a variety of instruments (written documents required to be recorded in a public office to give formal expression to a legal act or agreement which creates, secures, modifies, or terminates a right). Among these are deeds, mortgages, mortgage satisfactions, marriage records, wills, estate settlements, apprenticeship bonds, incorporations, and many others. As has been pointed out, these documents were once copied into books by hand or typewriter; they are now generally copied by photographic or xerographic means and then placed in binders. Once recorded, the original documents are usually returned to the person presenting them, though in some states it is customary to file the original documents also. The recording of instruments of these sorts has produced an enormous quantity of paper records, many of them in bound volumes of permanent value. Land records alone have taxed the capacity of hundreds of county offices throughout the nation. Because of the value of these and similar records, state law commonly direct that they be kept in "vaults."

Increasingly, public officials are recognizing the benefits of replacing their paper-recording habits of the past with a microfilm procedural recording system in which original documents (after having affixed to them validation and tax stamps, date, and sequential instrument number) are copied onto microfilm. Then, after the film has been processed, checked, and duplicated, the master negative is relegated to vault protection, a duplicate film is maintained as a reference copy, and the original documents are returned to the party presenting them for recording. *Voilà*—no paper copy in the recording office. The index to the instruments is fed into a computer, a computer tape periodically transfers the index to computer output microfilm, and the recorded document can be flashed upon a viewing machine within a matter of seconds, or at most, minutes: all this at a formidable saving in bindings, shelving, and space.

A microfilm recording system is also feasible for some records of only short-term value. For example, cities issuing large numbers of citations for minor offenses such as traffic violations are increasingly turning to microfilm as an efficient means of recording, indexing, and quickly retrieving data. By means of a fast rotary camera equipped with automatic feed, automatic document numbering, and automatic blip encoding, the original citations are filmed, indexed by computer (by, for instance, license plate number, microfilm number, data of violation, and violation code), and destroyed in accordance with an approved retention period. The microfilm then constitutes the official record and, because of its small space requirement and great convenience, may be given a lengthy retention period. Any new citations, payments, or actions are linked to the previous one by means of the index. A similar microfilming procedure can be designed for almost any type of current records, resulting in the virtual elimination of filed paper records.

An important technological development of the past two decades has been the link of computers and microfilm through "computer output microfilm"—COM, for short reference. This is a technology that can convert digital information generated by computers directly into microfilm images without an intermediate paper step. The economy of substituting microfiche for paper print-outs is enormous, and local government recording offices with access to computers and COM equipment have increasingly adopted the system for indexing purposes. After being fed into a computer, index data can be rearranged in a variety of ways, then converted to alpha/numeric characters that are displayed on a cathode ray tube; they are then photographically reduced and recorded on microfilm rolls or fiche. The index, periodically updated, provides instant recall by means of a simple microform reading machine. The cost of COM equipment—between $50,000 and $250,000—makes its purchase uneconomical except for jurisdictions handling about 100,000 or more original pages per month, but in many communities COM "time" may be leased from corporately owned units or service companies.

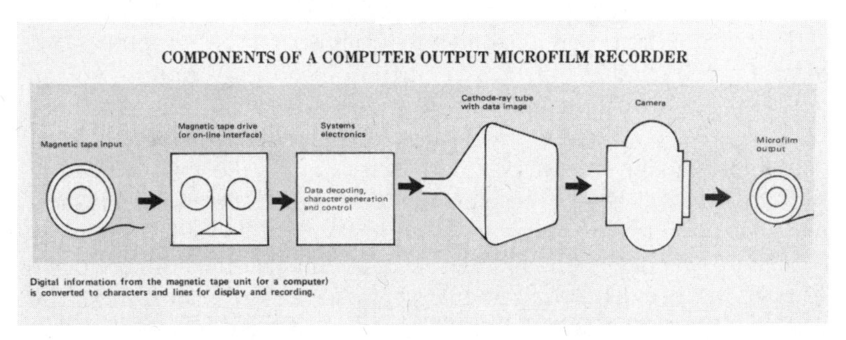

Fig. 20. Components of a computer output microfilm recorder. (*Managing Information Retrieval: Microfilming Records* [Washington: National Archives and Records Service, 1974], p. 37)

The high cost of equipment required for records programs involving advanced technology—microfilm, automatic data processing, and a combination of the two—suggests the possibility of facilities shared by governmental jurisdictions. A county government, for instance, unable to invest so heavily in the required apparatus, might contract with one or more nearby cities (or counties) to establish the requisite capability. Marion County, Oregon, for example, shares a computer with the city of Salem, its county seat. Many counties and cities "buy time" on computers owned by local banks or universities. Intergovernmental co-operation, as well as co-operation with corporate enterprises, can broaden the potentials for economy in many local governments.

Questions to be considered in planning a microfilm program are too numerous and complex to be discussed in detail here, but several generalizations are in order:

1. The judicious use of microfilm can help alleviate the problem of accumulated records—that is, existing records—with lengthy retention periods. All or practically all states have legalized the use of microphotographic copies in lieu of originals in most instances, though the microfilming of documents does not in itself carry authorization for the destruction of the originals. Indeed, most state archival agencies require the permanent retention of original minutes, deed books, will books, and a considerable number of other local government records. In these cases, the state archives or a regional repository under the jurisdiction of the state archives will usually accept the original records for preservation and use. *No public record, even if filmed, may be destroyed or otherwise disposed of unless such destruction or disposition has been authorized by statute or approved by the state archivist.*

2. A microfilm program, sometimes in linkage with computers, appears to be justified for many current recording applications on grounds of both economy and preservation. Microfilm technology has made significant advances, and public acceptance is growing. The mistakes made in the industry's "hard sell" during the previous thirty years may in fact have been blessings in disguise, for the disillusionment cast upon microfilm forced the industry, with the aid of archivists and records management specialists, to attempt more conscientiously to meet the peculiar requirements of public records programs. The respectability of microfilm has been greatly enhanced by a remarkably exhaustive study conducted in 1976 by the National Center for State Courts, whose summary report, *Microfilm and the Courts: Guide for Court Managers,* is the best primer available on the subject.

3. Prior to a local government's commitment to a microfilm program, the matter should be discussed with the state archivist. His office should be a clearinghouse for information on programs throughout the state, and his experience will often be valuable to local officials. A number of states have adopted statewide standards and procedures for microfilming, including Nebraska, whose state records administrator is not located in the state archival agency.[6] Regardless of whether there

6. Rule No. 7, "Microfilm Standards," is published in *Rules and Regulations of the State Records Administrator of the State of Nebraska* (reissued 1975). Two other helpful booklets published by the same officer are *An Introduction to Microfilm for Local Government Agencies* (1978) and *Microfilm Procedures Manual* (1978). Sections on microfilm are usually included in local records publications issued by state archival or records management agencies.

are state standards set by statute or regulations of a state agency, all government microfilming should meet the specifications of the American National Standards Institute.[7]

4. Understandably, in considering microfilming programs attention generally centers on the actual filming and retrieval process. Equally imperative, however, is consideration of preliminary and after-the-fact tasks. One of these—*preparation* of materials for microfilming—is overlooked only at the peril of the cost estimators. Preparation is not a great problem in the case of bound books and printed forms of uniform color and size, but it can be an enormous—and expensive—problem when dissimilar loose papers of varying colors and sizes and conditions, fastened by hasps or staples and perhaps mended by tape, are prepared for filming. High-speed rotary cameras are especially crotchety and may become jammed and damage documents that have not been carefully prepared. Special care, too, must be taken to film at the appropriate places target sheets and certificates of authentication so that the finished product meets legal requirements. A further expense, often overlooked in estimating the cost of microfilming, is the personnel time required to inspect the processed film to assure that every document was filmed, that each image is in focus, and that the film has a satisfactory density[8]—a slow, tiresome, eye-straining task involving inspection of each exposure to assure a quality finished product. Omitted documents or unsatisfactory images must be refilmed and the new images spliced into the master negative. This is expensive; it also adds undue delicacy to the negative, which is much more susceptible to damage and deterioration than unspliced film.

5. To the cost of the production of a quality microfilm copy must be added the cost of providing archival storage for the original negative. Even properly exposed, developed, and washed silver film is susceptible to deterioration from a variety of enemies such as heat, humidity, polluted air, and fungi, in addition to the normal hazards of fire and water. These dangers can be minimized, however, under strict storage conditions meeting American National Standards Institute specifica-

7. Among the ANSI publications needed by the manager of an in-house operation are PH 1.28, *Specifications for Photographic Film for Archival Records, Silver-Gelatin Type;* PH 1.41, *Specifications for Photographic Film for Archival Records, Silver-Gelatin Type, on Polyester Base;* PH 5.3, *Specifications for 16mm and 35mm Silver-Gelatin Microfilm for Reel Applications;* and PH 5.9, *Specifications for Microfiches.*

8. The National Micrographics Association's booklet MS 104, *Recommended Practice for Inspections and Quality Control of First Generation Silver Halide Microfilm,* is a standard reference for this task.

ESTIMATE OF MICROFILMING COSTS

	Est. Hours	Hourly Rate	Cost
1. VOLUME OF RECORDS TO BE MICROFILMED			
a. No. of sheets or cards ( )	—	—	—
b. No. of cubic feet of records (cu. ft.)	—	—	—
2. PREPARATION OF RECORDS (Readying records for filming, i.e., removing clips and staples, unfolding, arranging, preparing and inserting targets, etc.)		$	$
3. FILMING			
a. Operator's time	—	$	$
b. Equipment time (Hourly rate from Form 1, Item 5)		$	$
c. Film _______ reels at $_______ per reel	—	—	$
4. INSPECTION OF PROCESSED FILM		$	$
5. RETAKES			
a. Preparation of Records		$	$
b. Operator's time		$	$
c. Equipment time		$	$
d. Film _______ reels at $_______ per reel	—	—	$
6. REPLACING RECORDS IN FILE		$	$
7. TRANSPORTATION (Records to camera or vice versa)	—	—	$
8. TOTAL COST OF MICROFILMING (Total of Items 2 through 7)	—	—	$
9. COST OF MICROFILMING PER CU. FT. OF RECORDS (Item 8 divided by Item 1b)	—	—	$

Fig. 21. Labor for preparation of records for filming and careful inspection of the film for completeness and archival quality are among the major costs of a microfilming project. (Adapted from William Benedon, *Records Management* [Los Angeles: Trident Bookstore, UCLA, 1973], p. 169)

tions.[9] Some state archives offer free storage of local government security microfilm. When proper vault storage is unavailable either locally or in the state archives, a county or municipality may rent space for its film in a special vault administered by a service bureau. One thing is

9. See ANSI's PH 5.4, *Practice for Storage of Processed Silver-Gelatin Microfilm.*

certain: It is false economy to pay for microfilming records and then treat callously the camera negative.

A County or Municipal Archives

A records management program is concerned not only with monetary savings; it has a dual purpose of assuring the preservation of records of continuing value. Eventually most records grow out of their administrative, fiscal, and legal usefulness, but some of them continue to have value for secondary purposes of research. These records, scheduled to be retained permanently, constitute the archives of a county or municipality. These are the records that document the origin and history of the local government and provide the evidence of the development and operation of its agencies. They are the memory of the jurisdiction; they reveal a continuity linking the present with the past. They are so priceless that no money could purchase them from the poorest county or municipality, or replace them once they are destroyed. Their usefulness is discussed in Part II of this book.

The obligation of governments to care for their archives is so fundamental to civilized society that no argument should be necessary in their defense. Still, through neglect more than intent, thousands of governmental jurisdictions have countenanced the loss of much of their documentary heritage. The nonincendiary losses of the past have occurred largely because of the absence of active records management programs, for historically important records were often relegated to progressively less acceptable storage conditions where their condition worsened to the point that at best they were forgotten or at worst they were carted off and destroyed. Ironically, some of the current losses are being caused by overzealous records managers who too liberally and without adequate professional archival assistance schedule for destruction records of research value.

No blanket statement can be applied to all of the thousands of local governments in the United States, however, for in every state there are some counties and municipalities whose archives have miraculously survived virtually intact. For every instance of such great fortune, however, there are several others that have suffered varying degrees of losses from neglect, fire, or other causes. For both the fortunate and unfortunate counties and municipalities, the quotation "What's past is prologue" has meaning, because regardless of the care with which valuable records have been treated in the past, there is no longer excuse for their neglect.

In some states, particularly among the older ones in the East and South, permanently valuable local records no longer needed for administrative reference are centralized in the state archives. For more than half a century, for instance, the North Carolina Division of Archives and History has transferred valuable noncurrent records from courthouses and city halls, and the state archives is a veritable treasure house for historians and genealogists who come by the hundreds each week and who write as if the cost of postage is still three cents. The division has also microfilmed the permanently valuable records whose original copies usually remain in the localities (such as deed books), and reference copies of the film are available in the state archives, thus virtually eliminating the need for researchers to go to the communities to consult the documents. In younger states, particularly in the Midwest, some state archival agencies have established regional repositories for local records, usually at state-owned universities. Illinois, for example, has been divided into six regions with an authorized repository in each. Centralized accession records at the state archives enable a researcher to determine what records are available in each of the repositories.

Where prompt and efficient services of that type are provided by states, there is usually no need for the establishment of a formal county or municipal archives, for the needs of both the local officials and researchers from afar are more adequately met by the accumulation of records in facilities specially designed and staffed to service them. To be sure, the permanently valuable records remaining at the local level must be given proper protection, but that can usually be provided either in the creating offices or in a local records center.

Many other states, however, because of their geographical expanse, population, and tradition, have not found it practical to provide archival facilities for local records. New York is the best example: its rich city and town records would swamp the state archives, and even the idea of setting up state-operated regional archives may be impractical in view of the problems posed by the complex local-government structure of the populous state. There, the state archives provides an active records management program that encourages local governments to care for their own records properly. Considerable achievement has been made in that regard, and more and more towns and other jurisdictions have been made conscious of their responsibilities and opportunities.

Unfortunately, far too many states provide almost no archival encouragement or assistance to local governments. California, for example, has no comprehensive law affecting county and municipal records, and no effective program has been developed to provide practical assistance to local officials in the nation's most populous state. Even some states with relatively small populations, such as Iowa and Rhode Island, are without effective archival and records management aid to counties and municipalities. One of the great needs of the nation is for state governments to fulfill their obligations to their political subdivisions, for the losers are not simply the localities, but the people of the entire state and nation.

The absence of adequate archival facilities provided by the state places a direct obligation upon counties and municipalities to organize and preserve their own archival records. In the past, many conscientious officials have taken care of their records by simply expanding their vaults. The proliferation of paper records in recent decades has made that approach increasingly burdensome. Small jurisdictions may be able to continue in that manner, at least for a few years. The town of Half Moon, New York, recently occupied a new town hall with expanded vault space. Not far away, New York's county of Warren also has ample space, for the present. It will not be long, however, before populous local governmental jurisdictions will find advantageous a centralized archival repository for the permanent records of all departments. In a county or municipality operating a well-designed records center, the archives may occupy a special area of the building. In that arrangement, few additional precautions may be required (such as strict temperature and humidity controls and a public reading room). A member of the records center staff, exposed to archival literature and visits to the state archives, may double as an archivist. In other instances, an attractive area in the courthouse or municipal building can be fitted out for archival purposes and supervised by either a full-time or part-time archivist officially designated by the jurisdiction.

In some states, local public records are allowed to be transferred to a library, historical society, or other custody. That procedure runs counter to archival tradition and theory, for, under common law principles, public records should at all times remain in official custody. Under the principle of continuous custody, so forcefully enunciated by Sir Hilary Jenkinson in the first influential English-language book on archives administration, a public record loses its sanctity once it is removed from the custody of public officials. Thenceforth, a record out of custody is suspect, and its reliance in court is clouded by the fact that it has been in unauthorized hands. Statute law, of course, supersedes common law, and if a state statute specifically permits the transfer of public records to private hands, there can be only theoretical objection to the policy. Even so, questions remain. For example, can anyone but a public official (i.e., the legal custodian of a record) issue a certified copy? There is no problem when a record is officially transferred to an archives administered by a legally designated public archivist. But it is quite another matter when the record is handed over to a private individual or institution. Sound archival practice suggests—if it does not require—that when public records are transferred to a library, historical society, or other facility not under the jurisdiction of the county or municipality, the custodian should be officially designated as the archivist, thus responsible to the governing body of the county or municipality and, in effect, a public officer.

That seemingly technical point emphasizes the unique nature of public records and helps explain why, like other public property and funds, they cannot be disposed of except in accordance with state and local laws. It also helps explain why a whole body of theory and principles has grown up since the professionalization of archivists in the past half-century. This body of information is contained in literature published by the Society of American Archivists and other professional organizations and archival institutions and is essential to an understanding of the complexities of archival administration. Any local official, especially the records officer, involved in the care of permanently valuable records should be exposed to at least the fundamental principles of archives as contained in general works.[10]

These fundamental principles may come as a jolt to the average citizen, and they are too numerous and complex to be explored here. Perhaps four examples may be illustrative.

(1) In accordance with the principle of provenance, the records of one office should never be merged (i.e., intermixed) with the records of another office. This does not mean that series from two or more offices cannot share the same archival facility; it means simply that each series must retain its separate identity. For the purpose of description (i.e., a "finding aid" designed to identify and indicate the contents of each series), the office that created a record series (e.g., the county clerk)

10. Introductory workshops, seminars, and even specialized training courses are conducted, sometimes on a regional basis, by the Association of Records Managers and Administrators and the Society of American Archivists. Some state archival agencies also provide periodic training courses, and a number of colleges and universities offer either extended or short courses in archives administration. The most popular minicourse is a two-week institute, "Introduction to Modern Archives Administration," conducted periodically in Washington by the National Archives and Records Service in co-operation with the Library of Congress.

remains the primary control (or "author," in a library-cataloguing sense).

(2) Except in extraordinary circumstances, records should remain in their original order. Ease of access can be provided by finding aids. This principle emphasizes that public records were created and filed for a purpose other than historical research, and the arrangement of the records in itself has meaning. Documents thus have a relationship one with the other, and their physical proximity reveals that relationship. Death records, for example, are usually filed chronologically, and a subsequently prepared alphabetical index facilitates access to a particular certificate. If the original certificates were rearranged and placed in alphabetical order, the study of all deaths that occurred in a particular year would be all but impossible.

(3) Archival facilities require far greater security and care than are normal for administrative offices. Threats to records—fire, flood, vermin, excessive temperature or humidity, excessive light, mutilation, and theft—must be eliminated to the extent possible. Materials such as file folders and records containers should be acid-free; shelving should be of metal rather than wood; atmospheric controls should filter out pollution from the air.

(4) An archives is not a "dead storage" area; it is a functioning public service. Any "archives" without a designated custodian with at least rudimentary acquaintance with archival principles, available to make the records accessible to researchers on a fixed (even if part-time) schedule, is unworthy of the appellation. The archives should provide a pleasant, well-lighted study area, and copying services should be available.

In short, the establishment of an archives involves facilities, equipment, materials, and personnel beyond the usual experience of county and municipal governments. A commitment to such an establishment, therefore, carries with it a commitment to out-of-the-ordinary expenses. In view of the pricelessness of the documentary heritage of a county or municipality, however, the cost of its protection deserves high priority in the budget. After all, its archives constitute one of the few governmental possessions that cannot be replaced by the levy of additional taxes.

4

It Can Be Done

RECORDS MANAGEMENT remains unknown to thousands of local governmental jurisdictions in the United States. That conclusion —based upon recent observations in eight states, correspondence with officials in forty-two other states, and a review of the literature on the subject of archival and records management—indicates that the expectations of archivists and records managers a decade ago have not been fulfilled. There are many explanations, among them the absence of vigorous leadership by state archivists, records administrators, and their allies in the promotion of legislation providing improved statutes and increased assistance to local officials in connection with their public records; the continued diversion of the attention of local officials and their organizations to repetitive crises brought on by new programs mandated by the federal bureaucracy and local pressure groups; the penchant of budget officials to avoid the creation of—or to cripple existing—programs designed to save money and promote efficiency; the growing distrust of public officials that leads to more and more red tape, which, though designed for the protection of the public, may in fact result in the opposite; and the tendency of professional organizations to intrude into political and social concerns to the detriment of their chartered purposes.

True, several states in the past decade have strengthened their archival and records management services to counties and municipalities; yet they remain in the minority. Many local governments have, with or without state assistance, developed programs of varying effectiveness, but several earlier, much publicized programs have lost their initial vitality. In short, progress in records management at the local level has been unimpressive throughout the nation as a whole.

Yet progress, albeit far too limited, is being made across the land.

The brief case studies mentioned below represent only modest beginnings. But in the over-all national picture, even modest beginnings provide encouragement, for one step in the right direction may persuade local officials that reasonable expenditures on records management can increase efficiency, reduce record-keeping costs, and preserve precious documentation essential to the protection of the rights of both government and citizens. Programs of huge metropolitan areas have been excluded in favor of counties and municipalities more characteristic of the nation as a whole. Not a single program discussed below may be considered as a model, though that of the city of Portland may emerge as an example for other municipalities of moderate size.

County of Westchester, New York

Westchester is both older (created 1683) and more populous (880,000) than most counties of the nation, but in microcosm its documentary experience may be of value to younger and smaller counties. During its nearly 300-year existence, its records grew and grew, occupying vast quantities of space and demanding more and more equipment and physical facilities.

The enormity of Westchester's accumulation of records—nearly 133,000 cubic feet—became a public issue during the planning for a new courthouse. A records co-ordinator, appointed by the county clerk, spent some time in the New York State Archives to familiarize himself with archival and records management techniques, then conducted a facilities survey which identified 3,700 filing cabinets, more than ten miles of shelving, and an assortment of boxes and cartons filled with records. This initial survey revealed that (1) there was no countywide records management program regularly identifying and destroying records having outlived state-approved retention periods; (2) records of varying degrees of value were often housed in patently unsatisfactory storage conditions; and (3) the competing needs for space and equipment justified, even dictated, an aggressive program designed to dispose of records of no further value and to house and service those required to be preserved.

Following the facilities survey, the county executive requested each department head to designate one or more "records assistants" who, under the general guidance of the records co-ordinator and with the aid of an instructional manual, conducted a detailed records survey in their respective departments. More than 200 employees in 40 county departments participated in the inventory process, which involved the inspection of more than 16,000 file drawers and about 100,000 additional cubic feet of records on shelves and in containers. When completed in 1972, the inventory confirmed that thousands of cubic feet of records were eligible for disposal. Accordingly, after 1972, a large quantity of useless records was destroyed upon approval of the state archives. In addition, the inventory demonstrated that a great deal of space could be reallocated for more productive uses if the county built or acquired a records center for the housing of semiactive records of all departments.

Instead of constructing a building for the purpose, the county purchased for $750,000 an attractive one-story building formerly used by a book publisher. Located in a residential area of the village of Elmsford, seven miles from the county seat, this structure provided offices, workrooms, and a large storage area accommodating 10-foot-high metal shelving. The Westchester County Records Center was opened in 1973, and five years later it held 39,000 cubic feet of records from thirty

Fig. 22. Shortly after this photograph was taken, the "For Sale" sign came down, and this substantial building was converted to a records center by Westchester County, New York. The windowless portion is used for records; the well-lighted area to the right is used for workshops and conferences. (New York State Archives)

departments. Records with a reference frequency of no more than one per month per drawer are eligible for housing in the records center, and information is furnished to a requesting department by phone, or the original document is delivered daily by van. An estimated 67,000 cubic feet of records remain in county offices; thus the records center houses approximately one-third of the county's records inventory. The savings are substantial: in addition to releasing thousands of file drawers for reuse or sale, the center provides space at only a fraction of the cost of expensive office space. Furthermore, the records co-ordinator has the responsibility for assisting departments in establishing ongoing records programs, in disposing of records in accordance with approved retention periods, and in evaluating retained records for microfilming. Currently, however, the demands of the records center leave him little time for these essential tasks.

County of Allegheny, Pennsylvania

One of the most ambitious records management programs yet undertaken by an American county was instituted in 1978 in Allegheny County, Pennsylvania. With an accumulation of 270,000 cubic feet of records (a 100 percent increase in only nineteen years), this 190-year-old county of 1,600,000 inhabitants had done little more than worry over the absence of an orderly program for disposing of useless records and improving the quality of the remainder. In 1976, however, an aroused group of Pittsburgh business leaders formed the Committee for Progress in Allegheny County and channeled their expertise toward strengthening and improving the operations of county government. From "ComPAC" grew a Records Management Task Force to which executives gave six thousand hours of their time (plus sixteen hundred hours of staff time) to a forty-week records management study that cost only $11,000.

The task force observed records programs in nine other counties across the nation, consulted with state archives personnel, conducted a survey of the records of eighteen Allegheny County departments, began developing computerized retention/disposition schedules, and examined in great detail the county's real property records and documentation practices. Its final report, issued in January 1978, was a *tour de force* that simply but forcefully proposed radical changes in the county's record-keeping habits—changes designed to provide savings and/or cost avoidance of more than $1.25 million per year. Of the ten major recommendations made to the Board of County Commissioners, half had been implemented before the release of the final report; in addition, fourteen of thirty-one recommendations made directly to individual departments and row officers had also been implemented, and the others were in progress.

Central to the task force's recommendations was the establishment of a Bureau of Records Management to develop and administer a records program for all branches of county government. Staffed by a part-time director and seven full-time specialists, the bureau is specifically responsible for the development and implementation of retention/disposition schedules, operation of the county records center, operation of a microfilm service and review of all requests for duplicating equipment, development of a vital records protection program, and control over the design of forms. A records management co-ordinator in each department provides liaison between the bureau and departmental personnel.

The basement of the county office building is utilized as a records storage area with a capacity of approximately 30,000 cubic feet of volumes and boxed records. A comprehensive records management man-

Fig. 23. Phase one of before-and-after changes in a room housing records of Allegheny County, Pennsylvania. Next, see Fig. 24.

ual, prepared by members of the task force, is the official guide for all departments. It covers inventorying, scheduling, filing systems, records storage and retrieval, forms management, vital records protection, and micrographics, and contains a glossary and bibliography.

A second major result of the work of the Records Management Task Force is the beginning of an automated land-file system which, integrating all transactions relating to ownership, assessment, and taxation of real property, will bring virtually all land records into one place. By combining the technology of computers and micrographics, the new system is expected to increase efficiency in processing real property information, accelerate retrieval, free at least 20,000 square feet of space and much storage equipment, and eliminate (at a savings of $100,000 per year) the current indexing system. Three years will be required for full development of the new system.

Fig. 24. Phase two, records room, Allegheny County, Pennsylvania. (Photographs for Figs. 23 and 24 courtesy of George Louvris, Rockwell International)

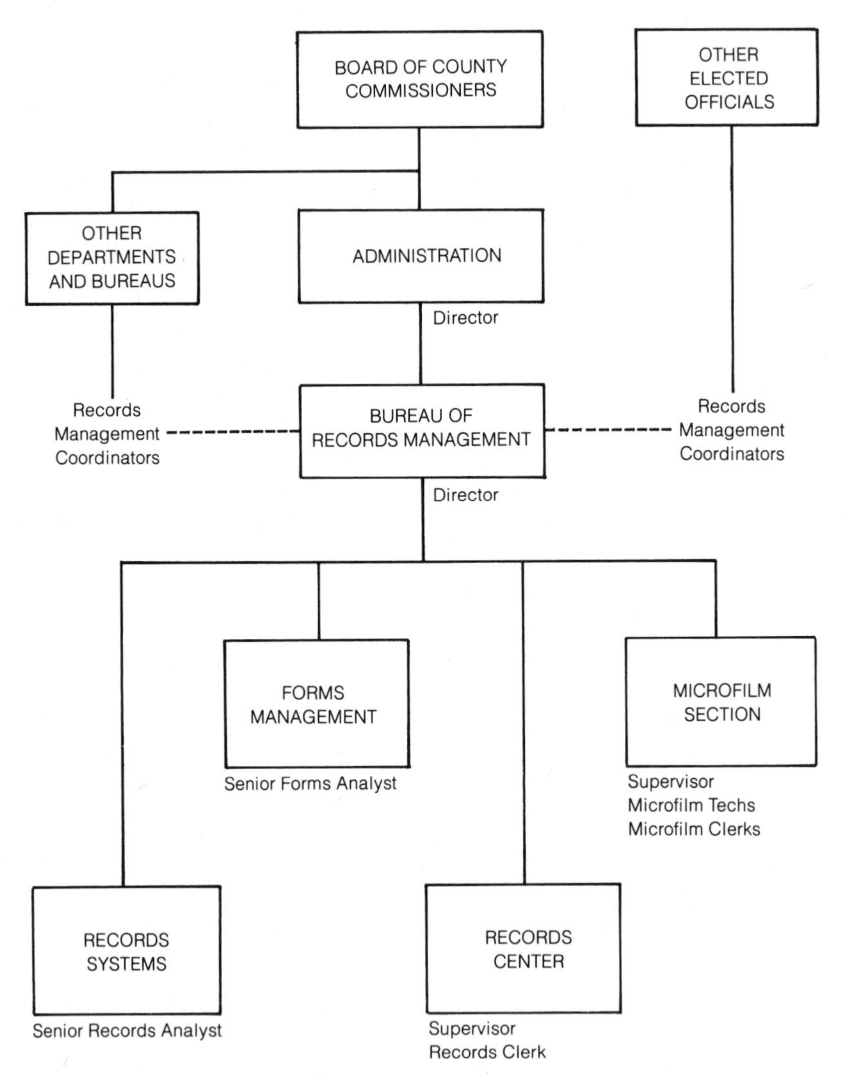

Fig. 25. Records management task force organization chart. (Adapted from *Modern Office Procedures* [October 1978], p. 106; courtesy George Louvris, Rockwell International)

County of Multnomah, Oregon

Multnomah, Oregon's most populous county, instituted a "records management program" many years ago, but an internal study in 1976 concluded that the resources of the program had been applied almost entirely to microfilming. The neglect of original records had led, the report stated, to "a growing, disorganized store of paper that is wasteful in the utilization of space and which is of little value because of the non-accessibility of particular documents." About 20 percent of the existing records were housed in an ill-kept warehouse, but the remaining records were still in the record-keeping agencies that managed their records "passively or not at all." The study recommended the reinstatement of positions previously cut from the program in an "economy move," the establishment of a program of inventorying and preparation of retention/disposition schedules, the outfitting of an efficient records center, and the adoption of strict microfilm criteria.

Just two years later Multnomah County received the achievement award for records management from the National Association of Counties. The award carries a lesson for other counties and municipalities: Substantial results *can* be accomplished quickly in a records management program.

This recognition resulted from the conversion of a single-focus program into one attacking the county's aggravated records problems through retention/disposition schedules, more efficient records storage procedures and facilities, and stricter criteria for microfilming. Except for the expenditure of approximately $238,000 for the remodeling and installation of shelving in a former Ford assembly plant for use as a records center and microfilm section, the expanded program required only a modest budget increase. The records center, equipped with open-type steel shelving 30 by 42 by 78½ inches high, has a capacity of approximately 12,000 cubic feet, now two-thirds filled. Administrative procedures, promulgated by the board of county commissioners, provide easily understood instructions for departmental records coordinators who are responsible for the preparation of inventories and proposed retention/disposition schedules, the preparation of files for transfer to the records center, and the application of improved management techniques to records within their respective departments.

The county records manager, who was professionally trained in the Oregon State Archives, reports to the administrative assistant to the director of the Department of Administrative Services and supervises a staff of twelve persons. Of these, nine are engaged in microfilm operations; the other three administer the records center and perform records management functions, including the preparation of inventories in various offices. More than twenty tons of records have been disposed of, and about 40 percent of the county's records are under retention/disposition schedules. Thus much has been accomplished, but much remains to be done to provide for each department an organized system of filing and indexing and a regular program of destruction of valueless records.

County of Jackson, Missouri

Prior to 1975 the condition of the noncurrent records of Jackson County, the home of Kansas City, was not unlike that in many other urban communities without an adequate records retention/disposition program. Large quantities of semiactive records remained in expensive office space; others were crammed into storage rooms, boiler rooms, closets, and a variety of hiding places. Still others were piled up without proper identification and inventory controls in a warehouse—misnamed a records center—which was rented for more than $25,000 per year.

After contacting the Records Management and Archives Service of the Secretary of State's office, the director of records began developing a long-range program that included plans for a more efficient county records center. At first there was difficulty in locating a suitable fire-resistive structure with ample floor capacity near the courthouse. By coincidence, however, the board of elections decided to adopt punch-card voting devices to replace the old voting machines. The substitution of the new machines released 18,000 square feet of space on the ground floor of the county-owned elections board building, located only a block from the courthouse. That area was equipped as a modern records center.

In 1976 began the massive task of reboxing, relabeling, and transferring records from their previous storage places to the metal shelving of the new records center. Initially more than six thousand bound volumes and twelve thousand cubic feet of records were moved, but in the process a large quantity of records was identified as eligible for destruction, and, with the approval of the Missouri Local Records Board, these were immediately disposed of. During the inventorying phase, many historically valuable records were identified, including a number of documents associated with the late President Harry Truman, who had served as presiding judge from 1924 to 1936. The merits of the program have been illustrated by the steady increase in the number of departments using the records center, where greater security, increased efficiency, and faster reference service are provided. The director of records also has responsibility for general office services, the recording of deeds, and the issuing of marriage licenses; too little time, consequently, is available for the application of professional records management techniques to all offices of the county. The functional records center, however, represents a first important step in a more comprehensive records program, and a records retention/disposition manual is being prepared.

City of Portland, Oregon

Three years ago the oldest chartered city of substantial size in the Northwest, Portland (population 400,000), had an almost unbroken run of records dating from 1851. That distinction, however, was something of a mixed blessing, for the absence of a systematic program allowing the disposal of useless records resulted in conditions described as "approaching almost unmanageable proportions." In short, the chaff was concealing the wheat.

In 1976 the city contracted with the National Archives and Records Service for consultative assistance in the development of a citywide records management program extending to the "entire information life-cycle—from creation to use, maintenance, and disposition." More specifically, subjects to be covered in the program are records inventory, records schedules, records center, files manual, vital records, microfilm appraisal, forms control, and word processing. A professionally trained records manager was hired on the city auditor's payroll, and an advisory committee was appointed, consisting of the state archivist, director of the Oregon Historical Society, city attorney, director of management services, and records manager of the port of Portland.

The records manager trained staff members and a group of temporary CETA employees to conduct records inventories that identified 5,640 different files. Series information was recorded on a direct computer input form. Following completion of the inventory, proposed retention/disposition schedules were prepared and submitted to city operational managers and the state archivist for approval. Within a year of the beginning of the inventory, fifteen hundred cubic feet of useless records had been destroyed and most of the permanently valuable materials (estimated at twenty-five hundred cubic feet) had been identified. The remaining approximately thirty thousand cubic feet constituted records that will be scheduled for disposition.

The city in 1978 was awarded a $56,000 grant from the National Historical Publications and Records Commission for the first year of a three-year project to develop "a model urban archives program." The grant, according to the NHPRC, is "not only to preserve and make accessible records of historical value, but also to improve records-scheduling and develop an automated information retrieval system." The project, the commission predicted, "will demonstrate to urban administrators as well as to scholarly researchers the benefits of soundly developed archival-records programs in large cities."

Both the records management program and the archival project, partially funded by the NHPRC grant, are currently under way. A *Records Management Manual,* containing citywide retention/disposition schedules, files maintenance procedures, and microfilm evaluation, is planned for release in 1979, and during the fiscal year six thousand additional cubic feet of records are expected to be destroyed under approved schedules. Other goals for the year are workshops for employees on the subjects of files maintenance, implementation of the schedules, handling confidential records, and development of microfilm procedures. A long-range goal is the integration of the records management program into the city's total information system. Meanwhile, the permanently valuable records are being transferred to the city archives for arrangement, description, and shelving. Implementation of SPINDEX III, a description and retrieval system for archival materials, is under way. A procedures manual for the newly established archives is planned.

If the objectives of both the records management and archival projects in Portland are achieved, that city's experience may indeed provide a model study for other local governmental jurisdictions in the nation. Success, however, depends upon the continuity of funding, a strong commitment by the city administration, and the acceptance of the programs in all departments of city government.

City of Long Beach, California

The city of Long Beach (population 400,000) initiated a records management program in 1972 and, though its staff was reduced from three to one in an economy move in 1977, its purposes remain: to promote more efficient and effective record-keeping procedures through the use of records retention schedules, forms control, and microfilm; to provide technical assistance, guidelines, and procedures to the various departments in the areas of record-keeping, filing equipment, microfilm applications, and hardware; and to assist departments with the disposition, destruction, and storage of records. Its trinitarian objectives are to save space, money, and time, while at the same time assuring the preservation of records of continuing value.

In 1973 the city council amended the municipal code by incorporating sections on records retention that authorized the preparation of records retention/disposition schedules. The inventories are conducted by the staffs of the separate departments, and the retention/disposition schedules are prepared with the assistance of the records center officer (a deputy city clerk) and submitted to the city attorney for approval before being presented to the city council for adoption. Schedules, however, do not provide for automatic destruction upon the termination of a retention period, for each department submits through the city attorney to the city council an annual one-time destruction request.

Achievements of the Long Beach program have been impressive: Since 1972, inventories and records retention/disposition schedules have been completed for eighteen departments representing approximately 60 percent of the city's accumulation of records. More than five thousand cubic feet of records have been destroyed, two million documents have been microfilmed, and ten thousand cubic feet of records have been transferred to the records center, administered by the city clerk and located in the basement of the new city hall. A *Records Management Manual* lucidly explains the records management procedures, and forms control is encouraged. The task of maintaining the program, however, is dependent upon the city's reinstatement of positions that were eliminated in an obvious case of false economy.

City of Bellingham, Washington

Bellingham (population 41,000) administers a modest records management program through its Department of Information Services. Since 1974 the records of all but three departments have been inventoried and placed under retention/disposition schedules approved by the Local Records Board of the state, and considerable quantities of useless records have been destroyed. The city records manager now laments that time did not permit the inventorying and scheduling of all records before other aspects of the program were put into effect—a lesson worth remembering by other counties and municipalities planning a records management program. The early schedules are now in need of revision because of the time pressure under which they were prepared.

The program includes microfilming, records center operation, and files management. The records center, with only 1,320 square feet of floor space, is already filled to capacity with records from all agencies except the Police Department. All records proposed to be destroyed must be filtered through the records center. It is anticipated that most of the permanently valuable records now in the center will be transferred to the state archives regional repository at nearby Western Washington University, thus freeing space for additional semiactive records. Some others are to be microfilmed. A standardized filing system has been installed in more than two-thirds of the departments, and a *Records Management Procedures Manual* has been published.

The experience of Bellingham, a relatively young and small city, demonstrates that achievements in records management need not be limited to counties and municipalities with massive accumulations of records. A program with an appropriate level of funding pays dividends in jurisdictions of all sizes.

City of Saratoga Springs, New York

Although the city of Saratoga Springs (population 20,000), which absorbed the earlier village and town, does not have a functioning records management program, it is aware of the unusual interest in the resort community's permanently valuable records and has used a novel approach to provide for their preservation and use.

By means of community development funds, the city has restored Drink Hall—the old trolley station—and fitted out a portion of it as a city archives. A vault (with a capacity of four hundred cubic feet of records), an office for the city historian, and a study area are provided. A small grant from the National Historical Publications and Records Commission furnished a temporary archivist to assist Mrs. Beatrice Sweeney, city historian, in the selection, transfer, arrangement, and description of the records, with the advice of the staff of the New York State Archives. The city archives, to be open on a regular part-time schedule, combines protective facilities with rare visibility, for Drink Hall serves as a sort of reception center for the historic community.

An inspection of the city hall revealed a substantial amount of ill-used space on its top floor, which, with the installation of climate controls and shelving, could serve efficiently as a small records center for the removal of semiactive records from crowded office spaces.

City of Schenectady, New York

The city of Schenectady (population 80,000) shares the advantage of no significant loss of records with the disadvantage of difficulty in locating specific documents. Some progress is being made, however, with the creation of a records management committee and the hiring of several temporary employees with Comprehensive Employment and Training Act funds. Many records series have been inventoried and some disposal has been approved. A portion of the top floor of the city hall has been set aside for records storage, various departments being assigned wired-off cages. As usually happens in such arrangements, however, nonrecord materials are allowed and the spaces tend to become little more than storage bins. A more efficient use can be made of the floor as a records center by the installation of climate controls and shelving.

On the same floor is a history center, which is less an archives than a collection of local materials, public and private, including museum items. The city is large enough to warrant the employment of a professional archivist who could double as city records officer and archivist. The city received a $1,750 grant from the National Historical Publications and Records Commission to microfilm the minutes of the city council for the period 1798–1905.

Town of New Castle, New York

The handsome New Castle Town Hall in Horace Greeley's home community of Chappaqua inexplicably provides no fireproof vault; instead, some of the older archival materials are kept in standing safes. Useless records are disposed of in accordance with state archives approval, and a basement storeroom houses some semiactive records, but there is no formal records management program. New Castle is probably typical of hundreds of other towns in the Northeast that have avoided serious records-space problems simply by building larger quarters as needed. In one respect, however, the town is atypical. During the bicentennial of the American Revolution, many of the rich historical documents of New Castle and its mother town, North Castle, for the period from 1736 to 1850 were copied and edited by Mrs. Frances Cook Lee, the town historian. Generously illustrated and incorporating additional materials, the two published volumes provide graphic proof of the dedication of successive town clerks who have cared for the archives the past 250 years. The publication also demonstrates, far better than archival theory can do, the immense pride that a community can share when its most important records are not only preserved but are also selectively printed for the education and enjoyment of the citizens. The people of New Castle now know that history is more interesting than fiction.

5

The Future of Local Records Management

THE snail's pace of progress in the development of local records programs during the past decade offers little optimism that more substantial accomplishments lie ahead. The impending revolt of the taxpayers against bureaucratic waste, however, may generate an unforeseen impetus for government at all levels to include a vigorous records management program in broader efforts to put reins upon unnecessary spending.

The growing public resentment against inefficiency provides archivists and records managers—and all others aware of the false economy in harboring useless records—with a ready-made issue. A logical, forceful appeal for an efficient records program is more apt than ever to convince hardpressed county and municipal officials that records management makes sense and saves cents—even saves thousands of dollars. Perhaps the time may come when it will be indefensible for local governments to *avoid* a positive program of records management. If such acceptance of the importance of records management becomes widespread, by what means will it have occurred?

1. *By the initiative of alert public officials whose administrative acumen leads them to question the inevitability of uncontrolled growth of records.* There is nothing mysterious about good records management; it grows out of good administration. Records differ from other public property mainly in two ways: records are organic in nature (i.e., they grow somewhat like an organism, producing a consequential relationship between individual documents comprising a records series); and records have a protective purpose (i.e., records protect the rights of both individual citizens and their government and therefore are controlled by laws and traditions that prohibit their disposal except in

accordance with strict procedures). If these special characteristics of records appear to complicate development of an orderly program of keeping and disposing of public records, it should be remembered that county and municipal governments routinely handle even more complex responsibilities. For instance, garbage collection requires the selection of personnel and equipment and the determination of disposal procedures with special care to avoid a threat to public health and the community's senses of smell and appearance. Certainly a records management program requires no more intellectual exercise than the collection and disposition of garbage; it requires simply a different kind of intellectual control. It is no more incongruous for a local government to engage an archivist or records manager to supervise the disposition of its records than it is to employ a sanitary engineer to supervise the disposition of its garbage. Once records management is accepted as a sensible and economical role of government, it can take its place alongside other essential functions such as auditing, reporting, and budgeting—and garbage disposal.

2. *By leadership from state archival agencies.* The Supreme Court in repeated decisions (the one person-one vote edict, for instance) has ruled that counties and municipalities are creatures of the states. The states, therefore, have an obligation not only to provide statutory controls over local records but also to advise and assist local governments in the implementation of the laws. The repetitious lamentations in this book are sad reminders that too few states are fulfilling these responsibilities. Some are without even a comprehensive records act; some have a public records act but no state program to implement it; and even those with both laws and programs are proficient only in limited phases of records management. Not a single state in the Union can be said to administer a program that provides *all* levels of local government with adequate guidance and assistance.

The absence or weakness of state programs can be laid at the feet of specialists in the archival and records management fields. Legislatures are responsive to demonstrated needs, and individual legislators are no more difficult to convince of the merits of practical and economical programs than neighbors next door. Too many archivists and records managers have limited their energies to their professional work and organizations, hiding their lights under a bushel at the state level. The stereotype of the archivist and his musty archives is indeed unjustified, but until state archivists and records managers are willing to promote vigorously the concept of records management in the courthouses, city halls, legislative halls, and committee rooms, their effectiveness in providing comprehensive services to local governments will be severely limited. Records management is not difficult to "sell" when the concept is couched in terms easily understood by the laity. The place to start is at the local level. Custodians of records are seldom willing to be dictated to, but the vast majority of them welcome state assistance when it is offered in a spirit of public service. A well-planned proposal—one that genuinely seeks to bring the state archivist into a partnership with local custodians for the benefits of society in general—will find support from county and municipal officials. Their annual associational meetings, at which the state archivist should be as familiar as their own members, are logical forums for discussion of the need for records management programs. North Carolina's experience is ample evidence that a county records program, initially drafted by the state archivist, will win the overwhelming support of statewide associations of county officials when they are invited to assist in the modification of the program and in sponsoring it in the legislature.[1] State archivists and records managers do not need to become politicians, but they do need to understand and practice good public relations. Most of all, they must demonstrate that they can provide to counties and municipalities services that will improve the quality and lessen the cost of governmental administration, while, at the same time, preserving records of continuing value.

At minimum, a state program should include a comprehensive state records act and an agency staffed by professionally trained personnel to implement provisions of the act. The extent of services offered to local governments by an archival agency may vary greatly from state to state, depending upon local governmental organization, the size and population of the state, and the tradition of relationships between state and local governments. In some states these services may be largely of an advisory type, with the staff of the state archives serving as consultants to counties and municipalities, advising in the establishment of local records management programs and approving retention periods. In other states, the services may be considerably broader, including the

1. The development of the North Carolina program, which involved county officials throughout the state, is traced in John Alexander McMahon, "A County Official Looks at a State-Supervised County Records Program," *American Archivist* 25 (April 1962): 211–218; H. G. Jones, "North Carolina's Local Records Program," *American Archivist* 24 (January 1961): 25–41; and Frank D. Gatton, "The Local Records Program," *Records Management Quarterly* 7 (January 1973): 12–15, 22. While this program has made significant progress in relation to county records, it has provided less assistance to municipalities.

Fig. 26. The North Carolina Department of Archives and History inaugurated a state-funded records assistance program for local governments in 1959. (North Carolina Division of Archives and History. Photograph by Charles A. Clark)

preparation of inventories and retention/disposition schedules by the state staff, the offering of substantive assistance in both routine and specialized areas of records management, the publication of a detailed records management manual, the acceptance of permanently valuable local records in the state archives or regional repositories administered by the state archives, and the microfilming (for security and/or reference) of valuable records that are required to remain in county or municipal custody. In several of the older states, important and heavily used records retained at the local level (such as deed books) are repaired and rebound by the state. All of these services are provided by legislative appropriations in at least one state; some states provide selected services (such as microfilming of permanently valuable records) on a fee basis. Whatever the cost arrangement, the services should be available from the state to the extent that local governments are willing to accept them.

3. *By encouragement or assistance from third parties.* Historians and

genealogists, acquainted with archival and records management programs in other governmental jurisdictions, have been successful in prodding states and individual counties and municipalities to action. In Tennessee a far-sighted genealogist initiated legislation that resulted in the preparation by the state archives of a county records retention/disposition manual; and in New York the wife of a legislator was instrumental in obtaining an additional legislative appropriation for the local records program administered by the state archives.

National organizations of public officials have from time to time discussed and published materials on records management. The previously mentioned study of microfilm applications, conducted by the National Center for State Courts, is perhaps the most successful undertaking of its kind. Other organizational contributions to the general subject of records management include the *Management Information Service Reports* of the International City Managers' Association; *Technical Bulletins* and *News Digest Reprint Series* of the International Institute of Municipal Clerks; and articles and special studies published by the National Association of Counties, National Association of County Recorders and Clerks, and the American Association for Vital Records and Public Health Statistics. Even so, records management has not been accorded the importance that it deserves by these and other organizations representing public officials.

More influential have been the national, regional, and state associations of archivists and records managers. Of these, the Society of American Archivists in the past has provided the most effective forums and the largest and most valuable body of literature on local government records, particularly through its quarterly journal, *The American Archivist*. With the SAA devoting more and more emphasis to private manuscripts and university archives, however, the National Association of State Archives and Records Administrators may assume a larger role in the promotion of local government records programs. Although heavily slanted toward business records management, the American Records Management Association and the Association of Records Executives and Administrators—now merged under the name of the Association of Records Managers and Administrators—have provided leadership and published articles on local government records. Regional organizations of archivists and records managers, sometimes affiliated with SAA or ARMA, hold meetings and seminars, and a few of them publish journals.

As creatures of the states, local governments have traditionally depended upon their own resources and those of the states for the support of records activities. The default on the part of some states to carry out their obligations to their counties and municipalities has led to increasing involvement of the federal government in the area of public records. There is an element of unfairness in this trend, because states that assumed their obligations and developed programs are now having to help pay for programs in states that, though no less financially able, lacked the foresight and leadership to provide the necessary resources for improved local records management. Still, local records constitute a scattered but irreplaceable American cultural resource, and if federal bait is required to induce states and localities to identify and preserve their archives, so be it—until the consciences of the communities can be awakened.

The role of the National Archives and Records Service as a pioneer in modern records management has already been acknowledged, but in addition, NARS staff members have from time to time either informally or formally provided consultative services to local governments in the absence of state assistance. Its publications, too, though geared to the problems of the federal government, are often useful at the local level.[2]

Since 1976, the National Historical Publications and Records Commission has provided a number of grants for local records programs. There is in each state a Historical Records Advisory Board that reviews applications and makes recommendations to the NHPRC. Although grants under the program are designed for archival purposes, some of the projects—particularly those involving preparation of inventories and retention/disposition schedules—may have direct application for records management generally. Samples of NHPRC grants (in addition to those made to Portland, Oregon, and Saratoga Springs and Schenectady, New York, already cited) include the following:

City of Providence, Rhode Island: $23,350 for the inventory, arrangement, and description of the city's early records.

City of New York: $59,500 for the appraisal, description, and preservation of 20,000 cubic feet of nineteenth-century financial records.

2. Of particular interest are selected *Records Management Handbooks* on such subjects as records disposition, records centers, files and filing, forms, and information retrieval. Titles and prices may be obtained from the Office of Records Management, National Archives and Records Service, Washington, D.C. 20408, though the handbooks are ordered from the Superintendent of Documents, Washington, D.C. 20402. Persons wishing to read widely in the field of records management should consult Frank B. Evans, compiler, *Modern Archives and Manuscripts: A Select Bibliography* (Chicago: Society of American Archivists, 1975).

City of Kalamazoo, Michigan: $15,000 for the microfilming of selected city records.

City of San German, Puerto Rico: $4,200 to assist in developing a continuing municipal archives program.

City of Birmingham, Alabama: $9,000 for the inventory and appraisal of the city's records as a first step toward an archival program.

Albany County, New York: $9,235 for the identification of archival materials and the publication of an inventory.

The commission has also made grants to state agencies to assist in the formulation of programs of state assistance to local governments. One of these was a $20,117 grant to the Iowa State Historical Department for a survey, inventory, and preliminary retention/disposition schedule for selected Iowa municipalities. Another was to the Departments of Administration, Local Affairs, and Development, and the State Historical Society of Wisconsin for $53,415 for the drafting of retention/disposition schedules for municipal records and for the improvement of local records programs. Among institutional recipients were North Texas State University, which received $20,240 to continue the survey and preparation of inventories of Texas county records;[3] and Western Washington University, which was granted $35,000 to inventory the records of public utility districts in the Pacific Northwest.

Funds for grants from the NHPRC are limited, and the projects completed under provisions of the grants are intended to serve as examples of accomplishments possible in improved local records programs. Local officials may obtain more information about the program from the state historical records co-ordinator (usually the state archivist) or directly from the National Historical Publications and Records Commission, National Archives and Records Service, Washington, D.C. 20408.[4]

Few other federal agencies have concerned themselves with local government records programs. An exception is the Department of Housing and Urban Development, which in 1978 announced plans for

3. This unique project has published useful inventories of the records of many Texas counties. Each inventory contains a brief history of the county, a description of the duties of each office, and a department-by-department inventory of records. Series entries include the title, inclusive dates, quantity, arrangement, and a paragraph description. The inventory for Nueces County required more than three hundred pages in two volumes. Local officials in other states contemplating a records inventory may find helpful earlier surveys, such as those compiled and sometimes published by the Historical Records Survey of the Works Progress Administration.

4. Summaries of local records in state archival agencies are found in the commission's *Directory of Archives and Manuscript Repositories* (1978).

a limited number of grants to local governments for the development of model land title recordation systems. Federally funded employment programs, particularly CETA, have furnished personnel for relatively simple records work in many counties and municipalities. On-site observations of some of these activities indicate that satisfactory results depend heavily upon the adequacy of professionally trained supervisory personnel. Irreversible harm can be done by amateurs who, without a basic knowledge of the principles of archival and records management, are allowed to "straighten out" or "arrange" public records without strict professional supervision.

In the final analysis, local records management will be as good or as bad as the county or municipality chooses it to be. Local officials have a right to expect advice, encouragement, and assistance from the state archival agency, but the development and administration of an active, effective, continuing program—one designed to produce fewer but better records, to provide for an orderly disposition of records after they have served their usefulness, and to assure the preservation and use of records of continuing research value—will remain a fundamental responsibility of local government. In the American system, that is as it should be.

Part 2

Use of Local Government Records

6

Local Governments and Their Records

81,000 Repositories of Records

YOU may not know much about government, but your government has always known a lot about you and your ancestors. All the highlights and turns of fortune in life have long been recorded somewhere in the official records: birth, death, taxes, inheritances, licenses, marriage and divorce, property transfers, bankruptcies, and lawsuits.[1]

Well, not *all* the highlights and turns of fortune are recorded, but Tom Felt is essentially right, for there are about 81,000 units of local government in the United States, and every one of them deals in matters of concern to at least some of the citizens. And, since the modern bureaucracy simply cannot function without records, it is safe to assume that nearly all of these units of government—counties, cities, towns, villages, boroughs, parishes, court districts, school districts, fire districts, public utility districts, drainage districts, and other special purpose districts—create records that tell something about or affect the lives of the people that they serve. These records are created in connection with the day-to-day functions of public offices, but many of them—particularly those of older counties and towns—have value for purposes for which they were never intended.[2] They offer grist for the historian's mill. And what grist it is! Records of births, deaths, marriages, property ownership, settlement of estates, taxes, voting; records of ordinances and regulations, of complaints and charges, of crime and punishment, of trials and verdicts, of the insane and the destitute, of fires and floods, of plagues and quarantines, of behavior

1. Thomas E. Felt, *Researching, Writing, and Publishing Local History* (Nashville: American Association for State and Local History, 1976), p. 43.

2. For a discussion of the primary—i.e., administrative—value of records as opposed to their secondary—i.e., research—value, see above, pp. 43–46.

and curfew, of taverns and bakeries, of slaves and masters, of wives and husbands, of fences and roads, of earthquakes and wars.

Records of local government constitute America's cupboard of unspoiled goodies, often peeked at or smelled by the curious, occasionally fondled and nibbled by amateur historians and genealogists, sometimes prepared and served up on a delectable platter by scholars. A smorgasbord of manuscripts, the richness of which is concealed by their classification as simply "old records." These hundreds of millions of documents have suffered in varying degrees—from natural deterioration, from the elements, from vermin, from theft, from human neglect or deliberate destruction—but those that remain in the county courthouses and city, town, and village halls of the nation conceal the unwritten and unknown history of America. Taken together, their quantity and their characteristics are overwhelming—so much so that the absence of a comprehensive guide to local records is explained by the stark fact that there is too much variety in the organizational structure of local governments and in the types and quantities of records that they create. In sum, the subject cannot be encompassed in a book. At minimum, each state would require its own guide, and frequent exceptions to the general rule would have to be cited even within one state.

A brief survey of the development of local government in the United States may illustrate the tenuousness of generalizations on local records.

The American County

American local governments not surprisingly grew out of Old World influences, primarily that of the English. The colonial county was essentially a transplanting of the English county which had evolved from the medieval shire. As early as 1634, sparsely settled Virginia was divided into eight shires or counties, each governed by a county court comprised of planters appointed by the governor and serving as an election, judicial, military, and civil district. The shire-reeve (sheriff) was the chief officer. The county emerged as the most important level of government in the early middle and southern colonies and later in the territories to the west. The county courthouse became the focus of the individual citizen's dealings with the government. There the county court met as both the judicial and administrative body, dispensing justice but also regulating the lives of the people.

. . . the court in the earliest days regulated midwifery and provided for the registration of births. It then provided for the education of the children, and, likewise, the conditions under which they should be indentured as servants. It extended its protection to include others who were unable to protect themselves—illegitimate children, the poor, the insane, Negroes and Indians. It provided a means for the orderly distribution of unoccupied lands by registering claims and regulating landmarks, and then maintained men in their tenures with its process. The court also protected chattels by providing for the registration of brands. The court built highways, bridges and dikes and regulated fences and ferries. At times it even supervised the church, providing for buildings, ministers, and its collection of tithes. It assessed and collected taxes. It welcomed some into citizenship by offering a procedure for naturalization, and it cast others outside the body politic, by declaring them outlaws, who could be shot down on sight as creatures of the wild.

. . . A man's basic activities such as hunting, fishing and whaling were all regulated. The kinds of bread which bakers might bake were stipulated, the size and weight of loaves fixed, as well as the manner in which they were to be marked and the price at which they were to be sold. The leather to be exported or used for manufacturing purposes within the colony was inspected and stamped, and to use uninspected leather was a punishable offense. The wood to be used for staves and drums was all prescribed. Flour, tobacco, hemp and meat to be exported were regulated as to quality and method of packing. All of these regulations were supervised by the county court. Finally, for those who succumbed to this economy the court fixed a place of burial and guaranteed its inviolability.[3]

The county court thus in many ways regulated the lives of the people from the cradle to the grave, then presided over the distribution of their estates. In recent decades, counties have become increasingly important in administering public improvements, public safety and protection activities, and planning and zoning. A listing of its additional powers—passage of ordinances, issuance of licenses, regulation of behavior, appointment of officers, regulation of unfenced animals, etc.—would be lengthy. The points to be made here are that with the exception of New England the county is the level of government that most intimately touches the citizens, that modern counties still retain their primacy in most states of the Union, and that almost every power asserted by the county is accompanied by an entry into the records. The lesson is inescapable: county records in all but a few states constitute the most important historical documentation of the American past.

3. Herbert William Keith Fitzroy, "The Part of the Archivist in the Writing of American Legal History," *American Archivist* I (July 1938): 121.

In 1976 there were in the United States 3,042 counties, 23 city-county combinations, and 39 independent cities that provided services traditionally associated with counties.[4] Delaware has three counties, Texas 254. Counting Alaskan boroughs and Louisiana parishes, which provide countylike services, and the counties of Connecticut and Rhode Island that no longer have administrative functions, virtually all Americans live in geographical entities akin to counties. In size, counties range from 26 square miles (Arlington County, Virginia) to 20,117 square miles (San Bernardino County, California); but the North Slope Borough of Alaska contains 88,281 square miles, larger than the entire state of Kansas. In terms of 1970 population, counties range from 164 inhabitants in Loving County, Texas, to 7,036,887 persons in Los Angeles County, California.[5]

Towns and Cities

While counties served satisfactorily as the chief local government unit in other regions, geography dictated a smaller administrative unit in New England. The soil, climate, and relations with the Indians encouraged more compact communities; and the town—a descendant of the English parish that provided education, welfare, and roads in addition to its church duties—became the characteristic political subdivision. The New England town was a rural geographical unit, normally of twenty to forty square miles, often incorporating one or more villages. It performed most of the duties characteristic of the county in Virginia and elsewhere. However, Massachusetts did in 1643 establish counties, governed by justices of the peace and given responsibility for limited functions such as administration of courts, maintenance of roads, and issuance of licenses. Other New England colonies followed; but these larger political subdivisions did not attain great prominence, and two states have allowed their counties to become anachronisms. Like counties in most of the nation, towns in New England provide important documentation for a study of history.

New York adopted a middle ground in local governmental structure. It created towns that provided some basic services, but it also created counties with substantially more power than those in New England. Deeds, for instance, were recorded in the county, not the

4. *The County Year Book, 1976* (Washington: National Association of Counties and International City Management Association, 1976), table 2.

5. Herbert Sydney Duncombe, *Modern County Government* (Washington: National Association of Counties, 1977), pp. 1-34 *passim*.

town. An interlocking of the town and county was provided by the town supervisor's serving on the board of county supervisors (now usually called the county legislature).

The English borough was the precursor of the American city, another level of local government—a concentration of citizens responsible for their internal judicial, police, and other selected functions. It has been said that the United States was born in the country and moved to the city. If so, the move took a long time. The chartering in 1641 of the borough of Agamenticus (now York), Maine, was precedent for the establishment in the next three hundred years of thousands of municipal corporations that, deriving funds from markets, ferry docks, licenses, fines, rents, and taxes, assumed powers over their destiny in limited areas of government. Before the end of the seventeenth century, five cities had reached gigantic populations—Boston, 7,000; Philadelphia, 4,000; New York, 3,900; Newport, 2,600; Charleston, South Carolina, 1,100. By the outbreak of the Revolution, Philadelphia had grown to 40,000, New York to 25,000, Boston to 16,000, Charleston to 12,000, and Newport to 11,000; and by the end of the eighteenth century, "American cities had emerged as the crucibles of civilization."[6] Still, in 1790 fewer than 5 percent of the people lived in places with 8,000 or more population. Within a hundred years, however, the number of city dwellers had multiplied 139 times; and by 1970 fully 80 percent of the population of the United States lived in metropolitan areas.

Diverse Patterns of Local Governments

The complex pattern of local governments in the United States is aggravated by regional variations in place designations. To the everlasting bedevilment of students of history and political science, a small city in the South or West is called a *town,* a title better left to the New Englanders. And, to make matters worse, very small municipalities are often referred to as *villages* which, at least in New York, have a different legal status. These variations in local government organization, in fact, may best be exemplified in that state:

> New York is divided into 62 counties, and five of these comprise the City of New York. The remaining 57 counties are further divided into 930 towns and 61 cities. In other words, if a person lives in a particular county, he is also

6. Kenneth T. Jackson and Stanley K. Schultz, editors, *Cities in American History* (New York: Alfred A. Knopf, 1972), pp. 1, 43, 45, 49.

a resident of a particular town or city within the county; towns and cities are mutually exclusive, so a person can not be a resident of both. A town covers a geographic area usually of many square miles. In addition, within towns we find 550 villages ranging in population size from 200 people to as many as 40,000 clustered in an area of about one, two, or three square miles. It is important to remember, however, that a person who resides within a village is also a resident of a town. He is a taxpayer in both political entities and some services are provided by his town government and some by his village government as well as certain services rendered by the county government. Also within towns, we find over 800 fire districts, which are quite independent, and thousands of special improvement districts.

Superimposed on all this are 760 school districts whose boundaries are rarely contiguous with any other political unit; their boards of education, administration, and taxing powers are separate.[7]

Back in 1857, the Ohio Supreme Court attempted to differentiate between counties and other political subdivisions:

> A municipal corporation proper is created mainly for the interest, advantage, and convenience of the locality and its people; a county organization is created almost exclusively with a view to the policy of the state at large, for purposes of political organization and civil administration, in matters of finance, of education, of provision for the poor, of military organization, of the means of travel and transport, and especially for the general administration of justice. With scarcely an exception, all the powers and functions of the county organization have a direct and exclusive reference to the general policy of the state and are, in fact, but a branch of the general administration of that policy.[8]

Traditionally, the most important functions of counties included maintaining law and order, administering courts, assessing and collecting property taxes, providing public schools, conducting elections, maintaining rural roads, and recording legal documents. Thus the county remained largely an administrative arm of the state. In the past seventy-five years, however, the growth of the population and the changing role of government have transformed the county from a mere administrative arm of the state to a more autonomous unit of local government. Services performed by counties have been extended to programs concerned with health, mental health, recreation, parks, libraries, planning and zoning, housing, utilities, natural resources, fire

7. Kenneth L. Brock, "New York State's Public Records," *National Genealogical Society Quarterly* 64 (June 1976): 114.

8. Commissioners of Hamilton County *v.* Mighels, 7 Ohio St. 110, 118–119 (1857), quoted in Duncombe, *Modern County Government,* p. 34.

protection, animal control, mass transit, pollution, museums, water supply, elder citizens, traffic, sewage and waste disposal, civil service, and on and on. Counties have also taken on more and more responsibilities traditionally associated with municipal corporations.

These radical changes in the functions of governments, both county and municipal, have of course resulted in increased costs, more employees, additional offices, and changes in traditional ways of conducting business. The changes also have led to this comment: "County governmental organization is characterized by diversity, not only from state to state but even within states. . . . As has been aptly observed, if any 'principle' could be distinguished in American county government, it is the principle of confusion."[9]

Local Records, Local History, and Genealogy

Recent developments have of course been accompanied by changes in local record-keeping practices, two of which stand out: the great increase in recorded information, both at the county and the municipal level, and the introduction of new methods of recording and using that information. The growth of documentation results not only from the increase in the population, but also from the deepening control that government asserts over the actions of the people. One could conclude that government in the last half of the twentieth century has reverted to the colonial tradition of attempting to regulate both the personal and business lives of the citizens. The difference may lie less in the degree of regulation than in the unmanageability of the giant bureaucracy that does the regulating. However, the changing complexion of local governments, both in terms of population and structure and in the assumption of many traditionally local responsibilities by state and federal governments, should not obscure the important role of counties and municipalities in documenting the history of the nation.

The creation of counties and municipalities was an essential early step in the establishment of self-government in America; and often, from the very day of their formation, they began making records. The minutes of the first meeting of the county commissioners or city council or town board represent, along with the legislative enabling act, a sort of birth certificate; and these and subsequent well-kept minutes provide an abstract, a kind of table of contents of the evolution of the

9. Russell W. Maddox and Robert F. Fuquay, *State and Local Government*, 3rd edition (New York: D. Von Nostrand Company, 1975), p. 439.

community. Minutes, however, were not intended to document every detail of administration and justice, so correlative records were begun, often in book form, for ordinances, marriages, births, deaths, arrests, court dockets, deeds, wills, the poor, and a variety of other purposes. In addition, there were the "loose" records—petitions, warrants, summonses, inventories of estates, case records, and many others. The bound records comprise, wrote Philip D. Jordan, "a sort of town diary in which officials entered, some in flowing script and others with crabbed hands, village triumphs and successes, foibles and frustrations."[10] Douglas E. Leach added, with reference to New England records, "Great events such as wars, political upheavals, and religious revivals, colony-wide in scope, may not be systematically chronicled in the records of particular townships, and the researcher may have to scratch very hard to uncover significant materials on such topics. But if the purpose of going into town records is rather to feel the pulse of a community year after year, in good times and bad, and to see what were the problems faced by that particular group and how they were dealt with, then town records may prove a rich source indeed."[11]

The value of local government records as sources of genealogy and local history has been recognized for generations, and authors of thousands of books and pamphlets have drawn heavily from the rich reservoirs across the land. In the nineteenth century, the vital records (births, marriages, deaths) of scores of New England towns were put into print because of their usefulness in tracing family connections and identifying early patriots. Additionally, local histories began to appear. The disproportionate attention given to New England in early textbooks can be credited to the region's initiative in publishing and thereby making easily available in printed form its historical claims. As is pointed out elsewhere, the northeastern states were the first to take effective steps in the nineteenth century to require local officials to provide better care for their records.

New England's interest in genealogy and local history found competition in other sections of the country by the end of the century. The South, in particular, became intensely concerned with both state and local history, including genealogy. One of the reasons can be traced to the defeat of the Confederacy and the resulting economic and psychological demoralization of the people of the South. For two generations, Southerners could find little in their contemporary existence

10. Philip D. Jordan, "In Search of Local Legal Records," *American Archivist* 33 (October 1970): 379.

11. Douglas Edward Leach, "Early Town Records of New England as Historical Sources," *American Archivist* 25 (April 1962): 177.

about which to be proud. In almost every ranking of states of the restored Union, those of the old Confederacy were at the bottom. In such a position, people often turn to history to seek past glories about which to be proud. Patriotic organizations such as the Colonial Dames, Daughters of the Revolution, Daughters of the American Revolution, Sons of the Revolution, and Order of the Cincinnati—in addition, of course, to the United Daughters of the Confederacy and the United Confederate Veterans—grew rapidly. Almost simultaneously, history as a professional study was promoted by the proteges of pioneer "scientific" historians like Herbert Baxter Adams whose southern history "seminary" at The Johns Hopkins University trained early teachers of history at the college level in the South. About the same time, several states inaugurated ambitious programs to copy and publish colonial records housed in British offices in London. In short, history became, by 1915, a popular interest in the South, and that interest led to the formation of state archival agencies charged with protecting the records of state and local governments. More historical works were published in the region from 1895 to 1915 than in all the prior history of the area.

Younger states to the westward were more fortunate in at least two relative respects: first, their recorded history was shorter and therefore easier to trace; and second, the absence of masses of ancient records enabled custodians to care better for the existing records. In addition, the younger states generally had the benefit of newspapers and reasonable literacy from the date of statehood, and state and local histories could be based upon a wider variety of sources.

Genealogy has been called by Lester J. Cappon the "handmaid of history."[12] Indeed it can be, for genealogists tend to plow the fields from which historians often pick up arrowheads. A genealogical researcher thus constitutes something of a prospector, patiently sorting through masses of unindexed materials, digging out nuggets, and alerting others to the potential of the ore. They also monitor the care with which public officials maintain their records, and they often are responsible for the compilation and publication of abstracts of important local records such as county court and town meeting minutes. Finally, an increasing number of genealogists have progressed through the "tree-climbing" phase and now practice their craft under research standards not inconsistent with those of historians. In recent years leaders in the genealogical field have sought to raise the standards of their colleagues, broaden the vision of genealogical researchers, and

12. Lester J. Cappon, *Genealogy, the Handmaid of History*. Special Publications of the National Genealogical Society, no. 17 (Washington: National Genealogical Society, 1957).

improve the image of family research. Archival agencies, flooded with "genies," have in some instances conducted workshops, too often limited to instructions on how to locate specific types of information in the particular institution. A greater service could be provided by encouraging less attention to the construction of family trees than to a broader understanding of local history.

Use of Local Government Records by Scholars

Thus local public records, particularly those yielding information on individuals, have long been a standard source for genealogists and amateur historians. Sadly, however, academic historians have made less use of the rich archives of American communities. Hugh T. Lefler observed, "Of all sources used by American historians, local records are the most neglected."[13]

It is of course true that some of these records have been searched by scholars, and new light has been shed upon the past. Merle Curti and his colleagues effectively used the proceedings of the board of supervisors, dockets of the justices of the peace, and other local records in their landmark study of Trempealeau County, Wisconsin.[14] Jackson T. Main made extensive use of probate records, tax lists, and other local records in his perceptive book on Revolutionary society; and New England town records have been major sources for studies by Benjamin W. Labaree and Sumner C. Powell.[15] Sam B. Warner, Jr., whose examination of 23,000 building permits issued by three New England towns between 1870 and 1900 enabled him to trace urban outward migration, found that careful use of local governmental records could help counteract the bias of private sources that ignore that portion of the population that left little in the way of letters, diaries, and account books.[16] These examples could be multiplied many fold.

13. Walter Rundell, Jr., *In Pursuit of American History* (Norman: University of Oklahoma Press, 1970), p. 129.

14. Merle Curti et al., *Making of an American Community: Democracy in a Frontier County* (Stanford: Stanford University Press, 1959).

15. Jackson T. Main, *Social Structure of Revolutionary America* (Princeton: Princeton University Press, 1965); Benjamin W. Labaree, *Patriots and Partisans: The Merchants of Newburyport, 1764–1815* (Cambridge: Harvard University Press, 1962); and Sumner Chilton Powell, *Puritan Village: The Formation of New England Towns* (Middleton: Wesleyan University Press, 1963).

16. Sam B. Warner, Jr., *Writing Local History: The Use of Social Statistics.* Technical Leaflet no. 7 (Nashville: American Association for State and Local History, 1970), pp. 4–5. See also Samuel P. Hayes, "Archival Sources for American Political History," *American Archivist* 28 (January 1965): 17–30.

New England records have been more heavily used by scholars than those of other sections of the country. Among the reasons: travel distances between neighboring towns are not great, town records are seldom overwhelming in quantity and are often well kept and conveniently accessible, and many town records have been published and are available without sorting through delicate manuscripts. A more subtle reason is that graduate schools in the area do not deprecate New England's local history as being "provincial." Noting that urban history has been recognized in recent years as a suitable subject for serious study by respected scholars, Edward W. Phifer, Jr., wrote: "The New England villages and towns, particularly in the colonial period, have been zealously studied in the past fifteen years by young historians of unquestioned competence. Those young scholars, according to a leading proponent, Philip J. Greven, Jr., believe 'that historians must seek to explore the basic structure and character of society through close, detailed examinations of the experiences of individuals, families and groups in particular communities and localities.'"[17]

Demographers and quantifiers especially are turning to local records. So are social historians studying family biography and community history, which is often conducted by amateurs working under professional guidance.[18] A more highly specialized field has come to be known as "family history," concerned not with the history of a single family, but "with a great many families—that is, with comprehending broad patterns of family structure and change for large groups, or, potentially, for the entire population of a nation."[19] These specialists gladly use data revealed by genealogists, but they seek to utilize the information for broader historical purposes.

That local history, so long deprecated by scholars, has made some gains in respectability is also attested by the fact that, at the 1978 meeting of the Organization of American Historians in New York City, at least thirty topics concerned local research, ranging from "Class Structure in Nineteenth-Century Railroad Towns" to "The Transient Poor of Providence, 1680–1800." Commenting on an earlier meeting at which local history research was discussed, Ray A. Billington wrote, "They [professional historians] are stepping down from their ivory towers;

17. Edward W. Phifer, Jr., "The Place of the County in the Study of American History: An Appraisal," *Carolina Comments* 26 (September 1978): 122.

18. See David H. Culbert, "Family History Projects: The Scholarly Value of the Informal Sample," *American Archivist* 38 (October 1975): 533–541.

19. Kirk Jeffrey, "Varieties of Family History," *American Archivist* 38 (October 1975): 525. Since 1972 family historians have published at the Newberry Library, Chicago, a newsletter, *The Family in Historical Perspective.*

they are substituting for unsubstantiated theories hard facts culled from masses of data in state and county depositories. They are looking at the past 'from the bottom up.'"[20]

Political scientists, economists, geographers, and sociologists are also increasingly utilizing local records and local histories. Even some history thesis directors outside New England, who ten years ago would have steered graduate students away from "provincialism," now accept topics dependent upon local sources. One would hope that this change of heart did not result entirely from the imbalance between the supply of and demand for historians.

Prejudice against local history—or at least low regard for it—is not easily eliminated, however. The attitude is not altogether undeserved, and it is not likely to be diminished significantly until the quality of local history research and writing improves significantly, both at the amateur and professional levels. A third of a century ago Donald Dean Parker wrote:

> It is not, after all, the highly trained historian who will write the local history of each community in this vast country. Not only is the field too great but usually the trained historian is primarily interested in larger areas of research. . . . If the local history of the United States is to be written at all, it will have to be done by an interested, if amateur, citizen or group of citizens in each community.[21]

Because Parker is right, there is slim hope that one of the legitimate criticisms of local history will be eliminated. This criticism is that too often community history is written in a vacuum by persons "who still insist upon concentrating their attention upon a midget rather than upon a growing man—a man who, by necessity, must be a part of a social group and who is conditioned by a host of factors quite outside his restricted backyard." Philip D. Jordan continued, "The story of any locality, large or small, cannot be divorced or dissected away from its neighbors or from outside factors that have influenced it and are still moulding it. The local always is a part of something larger. To ignore

20. Ray A. Billington, *Local History Is Alive and Well* (Ann Arbor: Michigan Historical Collections, 1974), p. 4. Billington's optimism five years ago is vindicated by an increasing incidence of specialized articles drawing their data from local records. The *Journal of Social History*, *Journal of Urban History*, *Journal of Interdisciplinary History*, and *American Journal of Legal History*, among others, exhibit a growing utilization of county and municipal documentation in scholarly research.

21. Donald Dean Parker, *Local History: How to Gather It, Write It, and Publish It* (New York: Social Science Research Council, 1944), p. xi. This volume was reissued in 1979 by Greenwood Press, Westport, Connecticut.

this more complete frame of reference is to do violence to the local."[22] Ray Billington, emphasizing that "proper local history is not really local history at all," added that "Local history is not a microscope that narrows our vision, but a telescope that allows a clearer view of man's place in the universe of time."[23] On the other hand, H. P. R. Finberg reminds us that the telescope "is not the only instrument that will broaden our minds and enlarge the stock of knowledge: the microscope also has its uses."[24] Indeed it does, and the microscope skillfully used by a careful local historian may be as instructive as the scholar's telescope. For, while admitting the myopia of many amateur historians, we may observe astigmatism on the part of professional historians who view the world as one indistinct generality. It is true that local history needs to be written in the context of a larger setting; but is it equally true that a microscopic analysis of *real* communities is essential if broad generalizations concerning the society of the nation and the world are to be valid. Herbert Baxter Adams said, "American local history should be studied as a contribution to national history," and James C. Olson, in his presidential address before the American Association for State and Local History in 1964, said " . . . local history provides one of the essential keys to an understanding of our national history, and, indeed, to the whole history of man. Because of this, it is an important academic discipline, and must be fostered as such."[25] William B. Hesseltine stated the case more succinctly: " . . . local history is the fundamental basis of the American story."[26]

That "fundamental basis of the American story" remains untold because it is concealed in millions of documents in thousands of county and municipal offices throughout the country. The combined efforts and talents of genealogists, amateur historians, and scholars will be required to release the light that these documents can shed upon our American past and present.

22. Philip D. Jordan, *The Nature and Practice of State and Local History*. Service Center for Teachers of History Publications, no. 14 (Washington: American Historical Association, 1958), pp. 7–10.

23. Billington, *Local History Is Alive and Well*, p. 4.

24. H. P. R. Finberg, "The Local Historian and His Theme," in H. P. R. Finberg and V. H. T. Skipp, *Local History: Objective and Pursuit* (New York: Augustus M. Kelly, 1967), p. 5.

25. Quoted in Ray Allen Billington, editor, *Frontier and Section: Selected Essays of Frederick Jackson Turner* (Englewood Cliffs: Prentice-Hall, 1961), p. 25; James C. Olson, *The Role of Local History* (Nashville: American Association for State and Local History, 1958), p. 12.

26. Quoted in Clifford L. Lord, editor, *Ideas in Conflict* (Harrisburg [now Nashville]: American Association for State and Local History, 1958), p. 12.

7
Local Government Records in Microcosm

Because of differences in tradition, state laws, organizational structures of local governments, and duties of each local office even within a particular state, virtually no specific statement about local government records is likely to be applicable to all of the 81,000 units of local government in the entire country. These differences account for the absence of a comprehensive guide to local government records, and they explain the difficulty of preparing this introduction to the subject. Patterns are elusive; the exception appears to be the rule. Only an inventory of the records of a particular county or municipality can provide the researcher with a dependable guide. Even then, an administrative history is required for one to understand the changing nature, purpose, form, content, and location of individual records series. Their very organic nature, coupled with the shifting of duties from office to office and the individual interest and competency of the public officials having them in charge, add complexity to an understanding of local government records. Little of what is said here, therefore, is true of all local records in one state. Still, generalizations may be useful in calling attention to the rich documentary resources of America's counties and municipalities.

In the following discussion, the general nature of county, town, and municipal records will be reviewed, then special attention will be given to selected types of records regardless of their origin.

County Court Records

Until well into the nineteenth century, as has previously been pointed out, the county court—sometimes called the inferior court of common pleas, court of pleas and quarter sessions, board of supervisors or commissioners, or, in Louisiana, police jury—was the most important level of local government in all areas of the country except New England, where the town performed some of the services normally associated with counties. American counties generally followed the tradition of English shires or counties where justices of the peace, meeting four times per year, exercised legislative, administrative, and judicial authority over the citizens. After Virginia established counties in 1634, other colonies followed at an uneven pace. From three to fifteen prominent freeholders, chosen by the governor or the legislature and often called justices of the peace, magistrates, or supervisors, constituted in early times "the government" for most citizens, for it was the county court that most intimately touched their lives. The names, composition, and powers of the county courts varied from colony to colony and later from state to state. Their authority generally increased, after the middle of the seventeenth century, though in some instances limited powers were transferred to specifically designated bodies appointed either by the courts themselves or the legislatures.

The extent of the powers of the county court in breadth and depth is not easily comprehended today by Americans who have become familiar with (if not consoled by) a jungle of governmental jurisdictions, sometimes contradictory and nearly always intruding into private affairs. But a glimpse into the activities of the county court is sufficient to dispel the myth that there ever existed "good old days" when people were free of governmental control. For, even though most citizens were normally touched only by one level of government, many of their affairs were indeed controlled by the county court.

It was as the combined local legislative and administrative authority that the court most intimately affected the citizens. It nominated or appointed and then required the faithful performance of nearly all other public officers, such as sheriffs, constables, clerks, registers, surveyors, treasurers, tax listers, solicitors, patrollers, processioners, entry takers, keepers of weights and measures, wardens of the poor, superintendents of common schools, and superintendents of the public buildings. It levied the taxes for the support of local government and directed disbursements from the treasury, appointed overseers and required citizens to contribute their labor in building and maintaining roads and bridges, and impaneled juries for hearing civil and criminal cases and to inquire into the affairs of government. To buy land or cattle, a citizen presented the deed or bill of sale to the court, which, upon proving (certifying) it, ordered the document registered, then approved a mark or brand so that the owner could recognize his livestock in the open range. If a citizen wished to build and operate a public gristmill but did not own the proper land, the court could force another owner to sell enough creekside property for the purpose. An ordinary—or tavern—could be operated only with a license from the court, which also set the charges for bed, board, drink, and stable. A ferry might be operated only by license, and the ferriage charge was set by the court. The estate of a deceased person was frozen until the court probated the will and appointed an executor, or in the absence of a will, appointed an administrator, either of whom was required to carry out the directions of the court until all accounts were settled. For an orphan with an estate, the court appointed a guardian and required bond; for a poor orphan or a bastard child, the court approved apprenticeship to a master or mistress and monitored the relationship. It approved headrights, heard the oath of allegiance and gave citizenship to aliens, held hearings to determine the mental competence of citizens to handle their own affairs, issued quarantines and adopted ordinances concerning health and safety, approved weights and measures, supervised elections, appointed militia officers, monitored the treatment of orphans and apprentices by their guardians and masters, manumitted slaves in accordance with state law, authorized peddlers to operate in the county, set bond for thieves, and licensed attorneys and other professionals. In times of war, the court banished persons whose loyalty was questioned, and at all times it viewed itself as the voice of the best people.

The records of the county court consist usually of the minutes in book form, case or file records often folded three times and tied with a ribbon, and the judicial dockets and probate records. The minute books, though often only skeletonic in content, constitute an enormously important record—a sort of outline of the life of county government. Entries are made chronologically, and there is customarily no index. Their value is all the greater because there are no case records or registered documents for many of the matters that the court handled orally. The handwriting, spelling, and grammar reflect the literacy of the individual clerks, and the completeness of information reflects their patience, perseverance, and competency. In some counties, an oath was recorded in the front of the minute book for easy administering. In areas that barred non-Protestants, the oath sometimes included the statement that "there is not any Transubstantiation in the Sacrament of the Lords Supper or in the Elements of Bread and Wine at or after the Consecration thereof by any person whatsoever," and during the Revolution an oath of allegiance to the American cause was required. The proceedings of the quarterly sessions began with the date and place of meeting and the names of justices present, then followed the order in which matters were taken up. Some courts directed their clerk to prepare a calendar so that like matters could be discussed consecutively, but the difficulties of travel and communications made this impracticable in large counties. Although the justices were expected to read and approve the minutes of the previous session, accuracy was generally left to the conscience of the clerk. Often, however, rough minutes were later more carefully copied.

Without an index, county court minutes must be approached either randomly or chronologically. H. W. K. Fitzroy, in his tracking of Richard Crosby through the Chester County Court Minutes in Pennsylvania, found his efforts highly rewarding.[1] Crosby, who migrated from England in the seventeenth century, was a small farmer, an average freeholder. During the period from 1683 to 1697, he appeared before the county court fifty-one times, only part of them voluntarily. His name first appeared when he was appointed to collect a tax for the building of a new courthouse; soon afterward he was involved in a civil suit in which he eventually won title to some land. There were frequent entries concerning Crosby's service as a juror, as purchaser of or as a party in suits relating to land, as a witness to signatures, and in matters relating to roads. Though the records gradually revealed a man building his estate and participating in community life as an increasingly substantial citizen, they also pictured the seamy side. Once Crosby was fined for unlawfully putting up a fence "to the damage of John Martin in his swine," three times he went to court to collect money owed him, and once he was haled into court because he had not paid his own debts. His behavior repeatedly came to the attention of the court: He was charged with challenging a group of Swedes at cudgels; claiming that he and his son possessed magical powers; characterizing his host's mother as a drunkard and his wife as a member of the world's oldest profession; being drunk and abusing the magistrates; calling the grand jury "perjured rogues"; and threatening that "if either sherif or clarke came to gather the country levie of him he would be the death of him."

Thus the records of the Chester County Court say much about Richard Crosby, as they do about thousands of other individuals. But, in addition, these same records say more than any other documentary source about the people, events, and places of Chester County and the society that was molded along the Delaware River. For many hundreds

1. H. W. K. Fitzroy, "Richard Crosby Goes to Court, 1683–1697: Some Realities of Colonial Litigation," *Pennsylvania Magazine of History and Biography* 62 (1938): 12–19.

of other counties that are old enough to have been governed by a county court, records similar to Chester's have been preserved, sometimes seen by only a few genealogists. Concludes Fitzroy, "The thing to be marveled at is that social and economic historians have made so little use of the records of so vital an institution and records so rich in social detail."[2]

The early county court, in addition to the administrative and procedural authority already discussed, exercised judicial powers in most colonies and states. Usually there was no limit to its authority over cases involving slaves, but for free persons its civil jurisdiction was limited to controversies involving less than a hundred English pounds or so, and excluded from its criminal jurisdiction were cases involving capital punishment. Following the Revolution and the establishment of improved higher court systems, the judicial authority of the county courts gradually declined. There was a further erosion of the powers of the county courts as they lost the right to appoint certain local officials. Under the constitutions of some of the younger states, elected boards of county commissioners or supervisors replaced the appointed county court. For instance, by 1851 Indianians were electing not only their commissioners but also the sheriff, recorder, auditor, treasurer, surveyor, coroner, and clerk of the district court. Not until Reconstruction, however, were the county courts replaced in several southern states by boards of county commissioners. Thus the day of the powerful county court had passed, replaced by a board of citizens holding the purse strings but lacking strong control over independently elected officials such as registers, sheriffs, and county clerks. These changes, gradual in the North and West, sudden in the South, had varying degrees of effect upon county records. The most obvious effect was the elimination of the minutes of the county court. Because authority exercised by the court during its existence was now distributed to various offices and boards, there was no longer one "diary" for county government.

Perhaps the richness of the records of early county courts can be illustrated by a sampling of the subjects covered during the early sittings of the Court of Pleas and Quarter Sessions in Rowan County, North Carolina, in the 1750s.[3]

The most common entries related to the recording of livestock marks and brands, recording of deeds, probating of wills and appoint-

2. H. W. K. Fitzroy, "The Part of the Archivist in the Writing of American Legal History," *American Archivist* I (April 1938): 124.

3. The following items are gleaned from Jo White Linn, *Abstracts of the Minutes of the Court of Pleas and Quarter Sessions, Rowan County, North Carolina, 1753–1762* (Salisbury: Salisbury Printing Company, 1977), pp. 1-110 *passim.*

ment of fiduciaries, appointment or qualification of officers of civil government and the militia, levying and collection of taxes, reviewing indentures and guardianships, receiving of petitions for roads and appointment of road overseers, and trial of civil and minor criminal cases. Less common subjects provide a great deal of information on the settlement of the frontier. Although Anglo-Saxon names dominated at that early date, each year's entries included a growing number of German names, reflecting the stream of settlers coming down the Great Wagon Road from Pennsylvania. One of the court's early actions was sale of lots in the county seat on condition that each purchaser within two years build a frame, brick, or stone house at least twenty by sixteen feet with a good brick or stone chimney "and that the Purchaser of Each Lot Shall Inclose their Lot with Post and Rail fence or Well Pailed." A courthouse was contracted for, along with a prison, each to specifications so graphic that a modern architect can virtually redraw the plans. Ferry licenses were issued and charges were set: four shillings for a driver, four horses, and a loaded wagon; four pence for a man and horse; eight pence per wheel for a coach, chariot, chaise, or chair. Squire Boone (the father of Daniel Boone), one of the justices, was granted a license to keep a "Public house" at his plantation, and prices were fixed for bed, board, drink, and stabling ("Dinner of Roaest Boiled flesh Eight pence Brakefast and Supper four pence. . . . Lodging Each Night in a good Bed and Clean Sheets Two Pence"). A deed was proved for "the Congregation of the Part of that Society Called Desenters to the Lower Sett."

The stigma associated with a common means of punishment—the cropping of ears—was indicated in John Baker's petition in which he swore that in a fight another person "Through his Malliese Bit the under Part of his Lef Ear of." The court duly granted a certificate to prove to Baker's friends that his cropped ear had not resulted from punishment of the court.

Living on the edge of Indian territory, the white and black residents of Rowan County were insecure during the French and Indian War. An entry states that three Indians, representing the Sapony, Susquehanna, and Catawba tribes, applied for a pass to the Catawba Nation, "being now on their Journey to Conclude a Genl Peace with ye Cattabas in behalf of the Sd Nations and Also Presented 3 Belts of Wampum to Sd Court by which the sd Treaty is to be Concluded." The following year James Carter was reimbursed for furnishing bread, wine, and beef to Catawba Indians on their way to Virginia "for the assistance of that Colony."

Rowan in the 1750s was a huge county with no fixed western boundary; from it eventually were formed more than a dozen North Carolina counties and virtually all of the state of Tennessee. Its county court for a period of time therefore represented an area now inhabited by perhaps four million people. By extension, the county's early court records assume an importance belied by its present area of 517 square miles and slightly over 100,000 residents. Rowan is not alone in that regard.

Another example of local documentation may be found in Boston where the records of the Suffolk County Inferior Court of Common Pleas are "replete with literally thousands of itemized accounts, inventories, bonds, promissory notes and other evidentiary materials" from which researchers "can reconstruct the fluctuating business climate, interest rates, foreign and domestic trade routes, import and export goods, as well as the food, clothing, and furnishings used centuries ago." Robert J. Brink, who supervises a program designed to preserve the Suffolk records, adds that the documents are to modern historians "as fossils are to anthropologists."[4] David H. Flaherty found that these materials permitted him to study "the serious crime rate, the characteristics of criminal offenses of various sorts, criminal procedure, and the problems of law enforcement." He concluded, "In my opinion, these court records of criminal and civil actions constitute the single most important source for the social, economic, and legal history of the colonial era, yet they are still relatively unexplored."[5] Among the 360,000 case files are records of suits for debt against John Hancock, John Singleton Copley, and Samuel Adams (the latter was jailed for that offense in 1773); of the bankruptcy of Charles Bulfinch, noted architect and chairman of Boston's Board of Selectmen; and of the effort in 1848 of Benjamin Roberts, a black printer, to gain admission of his daughter to a white public school. Roberts lost his suit but helped win a larger battle seven years later when the state legislature banned segregation in the public schools.[6]

Finally, the great cache of documents of the Suffolk County court moved Hiller B. Zobel of the Boston Law School to write:

No ice storms encapsulated any 18th century town; no embalming ash has brought the Revolutionary days to us intact. But we do possess pieces of that

4. Robert J. Brink, "Boston's Great Anthropological Documents," *Boston Bar Journal* 22 (September 1978): 12.

5. David H. Flaherty, "The Use of Early American Court Records in Historical Research," *Law Library Journal* 69 (August 1976): 342.

6. *Boston Globe*, March 17, 1977, and January 11, 1979; *The Phoenix* (Boston), September 12, 1978.

past life, preserved without change, and lying, like the wall paintings of Pompeii, beneath a layer of dust, awaiting excavating. We call them court records.[7]

Court records, however, constitute only one classification of county records. A cursory review of selected inventories conducted by the Historical Records Survey during the New Deal era illustrates the variety of documentation found in the courthouses of the nation:

—Ormsby County, Nevada: two volumes of marks and brands for horses, cattle, and sheep, 1875–1923; another volume containing licenses for several "glove contests," including a boxing match in 1897 between James J. Corbett and Robert Fitzsimmons.

—San Francisco, California (county and city): 5,000 documents labeled "Old Wills Not Probated Saved from 1906 Fire"; 17 volumes of complaints against saloons, 1905–1919; three volumes of "List of Radicals and I.W.W., 1919–20"; two volumes of "Applications for Permits, Kinetoscopes, Panoramas, Museums, Skating Rinks, etc., 1908–9"; four volumes titled "White Slave Detail, 1912–15, 1920–21"; 19 volumes of records of San Quentin convicts going as far back as 1872; and 7,250 documents relating to assistance to Italian and Chinese families by the Italian Board of Relief from 1932 to 1934.

—Otter Tail County, Minnesota: a file drawer of applications for permits to hold public dances (including character references for the applicants); a volume of certificates issued by the State Board of Massage Examiners; a volume of allowance records for the poor, 1891–1896; a register of the poor farm, 1895–1917; a drawer of records of the county tuberculosis sanitarium in the 1920s; one box of prescriptions for liquor issued during prohibition; forty-one file drawers of ditch records after the turn of the century; and fourteen volumes of naturalization papers beginning in 1874.

—Ravalli County, Montana: two volumes of recorded grants under the homestead acts, 1879–1923; four registers of bounty certificates issued for the destruction of animals predatory to livestock, 1895–1932.

—Williams County, North Dakota: 2,700 documents relating to 1931 drought relief; 3,000 applications for wheat allotment contracts during the depression; 11 volumes recording the exhibition of skins of wolves or coyotes or wings of magpies for bounty payment; 9 volumes of state hail-insurance records in the 1920s; 2 volumes recording the

7. Hiller B. Zobel, "The Pompeii of Paper," *Boston Bar Journal* 22 (September 1978): 20.

sale of Christmas seals; and 1 volume listing members of the county reading circle, beginning in 1923, and a list of books used.

—Sweetwater County, Wyoming: nine volumes of hide and carcass inspection certificates.

—Assumption Parish, Louisiana: a group of records of the Sugar Cane Production Adjustment Programs, 1934–1936; a volume of insanity records, 1914–1922; and one thousand items titled "Free Text Books" relating to Huey Long's pioneer state program for distributing free textbooks, paper, and pencils to school students in 1933.

—Cherokee County, Oklahoma: one volume titled "Cherokee Allotment Record, January 27, 1909," giving name, address, age, sex, quantum of Indian blood, legal description of the land allotted, and a certification by the "Commissioner to the Five Civilized Tribes"; reproductions of plans for the Cherokee Council House, 1867; and three volumes of oil and gas lease records beginning in 1907.

—Osage County, Kansas: a file drawer containing grasshopper-control records, indicating the brands of poison used; another drawer of records concerning property inspected for bindweed; and a volume registering the variation of the magnetic needle since 1870.

The more common records found in the counties will be discussed later. The examples given above may suggest that, in each region of the country, records are created that reflect the peculiar concerns of its people—records that are sometimes unknown in other parts of the country.

New England Town Records

Although the county in New England provided the judicial unit and sometimes the probate court, it was the town that most intimately touched the citizens and consequently produced records of exceptional value for both administration and research. The nature and structure of the town help explain the types of records that it generated.

As William Eaton Foster, New England librarian and historian, pointed out nearly a hundred years ago, the town furnished most of the conditions for a unit of government: "Its territory is not too large for efficient combination and cooperation. Its population is, in general, compactly massed. Its citizens are a homogeneous whole."[8] The earliest towns generally were formed by a group of people who, some-

8. William E. Foster, *Town Government in Rhode Island,* Johns Hopkins University Studies in Historical and Political Science, vol. 2, Fourth Series (Baltimore: Johns Hopkins University, 1886), p. 6. See also Bruce E. Daniels, editor, *Town and County* (Middleton: Wesleyan University Press, 1978), pp. 3–11.

times for religious reasons, sought to establish a separate community in which they laid out a village green, built a church and meeting house, sold land only to their own group or to highly selected outsiders, and accepted the town meeting as their government. Their first official record was usually a skin-bound volume called the "town book."

The growth of towns inevitably led to a modification of the "pure democracy" of the town meeting, for an expanded population and changing conditions dictated a multiplication of officeholders. The French observer Alexis de Tocqueville noted in 1835 that there were customarily at least nineteen town officials:

> The selectmen are elected every year in April or May. At the same time, the town meeting also elects many other municipal officials to take charge of important administrative details. There are assessors to rate the township and collectors to bring the taxes in. The constable must organize the police, take care of public places, and take a hand in the physical execution of the laws. The town clerk must record all resolutions; he keeps a record of the proceedings of the civil administration. The treasurer looks after the funds of the township. There are also overseers of the poor whose difficult task it is to execute the provisions of the Poor Laws; school commissioners in charge of public education; and surveyors of highways, who look after roads both large and small, to complete the list of the main administrative officials of the township. But the division of functions does not stop there; among municipal officials one also finds parish commissioners responsible for the expenses of public worship, fire wardens to direct the citizens' efforts in case of fire, tithing men, hog reeves, fence viewers, timber measurers, and sealers of weights and measures.[9]

Each of these officials—or at least most of them—kept some sort of records. The town book, therefore, while continuing as a skeletonic outline of formal community action, was supplemented by other growing bodies of records created or accumulated by administrative personnel. In several states—particularly Connecticut, Rhode Island, and Vermont—the most important of these are the land records, for as new residents were admitted to the town and as children grew to adulthood, land was divided time and time again. Throughout New England and New York, vital statistics—births, deaths, and marriages—constitute a valuable records series. Other series commonly found in towns include records relating to taxes, expenditures, roads, schools, elections, the militia, earmarks and brands, care for the poor, and ordinances of all types. In towns that have remained relatively small,

9. Alexis de Tocqueville, *Democracy in America,* edited by J. P. Mayer and Max Lerner (New York: Harper & Row, 1966), p. 58.

these series may be virtually complete for two or three hundred years. In the colonial period, entries for almost any subject were sometimes—as in the case of Berlin, Connecticut—made in books marked as land records.

The richness of town records in the Northeast can best be illustrated by several examples.

A group of "novices" set out to compile a history of the village of Katonah in the township of Bedford, New York. History became alive and the group was "hooked as though by a drug." The leader wrote, ". . . our first sense of its [the original town deed's] realness came when we saw the manuscript copy recorded in 1695 in our earliest town book. Why, these *were* real men—they really did get together at Stamford and trade 'twelve Indian cotes, six blankets, 300 guilders wompan, two yard red brodcloth, six yard red coton, and more by exspences' for a good part of Bedford!" This revelation spurred the researchers to trace the development of the town from its very first deed through the selection of a committee to lay out house and field lots and the agreement that no house should be built on less than three acres, that no exchange of land could take place except with the agreement of the inhabitants, and that new persons could be admitted as residents only upon approval of the freeholders. The story of a community unfolded as more and more ancient records were searched. Bedford was more than a hundred years old when this revealing entry was made in 1784: "Voted that No Persons that have been Over to the Enemy Shall Come into town to Reside if Any have all Ready come in they are to be Imedietely Drove Out."[10]

In seventeenth-century Rowley, Massachusetts, town officials ordered that, because of the danger of fire, "all thached Chimnies in the towne shall be swept and all thached houses shall be swept" regularly until the first of May. The town of Wallingford solved a leak in the local mill dam by plugging it with cartloads of manure, an admirable solution to two distinct problems. An entry in the Warwick town meeting records suggests something about predatory animals, Indian relations, and the town's precarious financial condition: It was ordered "That pomham [an Indian] be paid out ye treasury of this towne what is justly dew by order of this towne for killing A woolfe if ther be money in ye treasurry." And a story hardly capable of being improved upon

10. Frances R. Duncombe, "Sleuthing among Town Records in Pursuit of Local History," *Manuscripts* 15 (Winter 1963): 13–15.

by a Hollywood script writer is found in the Providence, Rhode Island, town records for 1676:

. . . there came into this Towne One Chuff an Indian so called in time of peace, because of his Surlines against the English [.] He could Scarce come in being wounded Some few dayes before by Providence Men [.] His wounds were corrupted & stanck & because he had bene a Ring leader all the War to most of the Mischiefs to our Howses & Cattell, & what English he could: The Inhabitants of the Towne cried out for Justice against him threatning themselves to kill him if the Authoritie did not: For which Reason the Cap: Roger Williams Caused the Drum to be beat, the Toun Councell & Councell of War called, all cried for Justice & Execution, the Councell of War gave sentence & he was shot to Death, to the great satisfaction of the Towne.[11]

With the passage of time, entries in town records became less quaint, but not always less informative. After independence, state government loomed large in the lives of American citizens, but town government continued to dominate the day-to-day activities of the people of New England and New York. Into the nineteenth century the records of New Castle township, New York, contained a variety of entries such as these: "Voted that Abrm. Hyatt see to the gitting a Covenant Desk Made to put in the Recods Laws wrightings and papors" of the town; the birth of a female Negro child named Roose, belonging to Gilbert Strang, was ordered to be recorded; James Dickinson reported that "Two yearling Hiefers Come on and Into his Iclosed Land as strays one of the heifers Is Red the other red and White No Artificial marks As I have Yet Discovered"; the overseers of the poor were authorized "to hire [out] the poor Kept in any poor house or to dispose of the poor in any other way as they may Think propper"; eighty dollars was ordered to be raised to pay the "present Debt of the Town and pay the town officers the ensuing year" and fifty dollars was directed to be raised to pay for roads and bridges; and in an election the citizens of the town had voted sixty-five to twenty-nine against the issuance of licenses for the retailing of intoxicating liquor.[12] The records of no other level of government yield so intimate a view of the routine matters of community life as those of the towns of the Northeast. To be sure, record-keeping has changed in most towns, but whether entries are made by longhand similar to procedures of centuries ago or by

11. Douglas Edward Leach, "Early Town Records of New England as Historical Sources," *American Archivist* 25 (April 1962): 175–177.

12. Frances Cook Lee, editor, *Historical Records of New Castle* (Chappaqua, N.Y.: Town of New Castle, [1977]), pp. 92, 102, 157, 198, 227.

modern electronic devices, the information contained in the records is vital to the documentation of American life.[13]

Other Municipal Records

The character of county government outside New England and township government within New England traditionally has been quite different from that of cities, towns, villages, hamlets, and other units of government encompassed (in this book) in the general term *municipalities.* The boundaries are more or less permanent for counties and towns, and the services of both tend to be less concerned with the conveniences of the citizens than with the fundamental framework of government—or, as the Ohio Supreme Court stated in 1857, with a view to the policy of the state at large and for the general administration of justice.[14] On the other hand, a community is usually incorporated to solve problems that arise when it loses its rural atmosphere and people move into such close proximity that a different type of government is needed to protect them from each other and from the natural consequences of overcrowdedness. Incorporated municipalities are prone to extend their boundaries as the residents seek to escape the confinement of the inner city in favor of more attractive (and less crowded) suburban areas. Thus they commonly expand both in population and size.

The difference in the characters of counties, towns, and municipal forms of government was, of course, far more distinct in earlier times, and what can be said of the eighteenth century may be inapplicable today. In earlier times, the government of an incorporated village usually did not take over functions performed by the county or town; it simply supplemented them. As a village grew into a city and perhaps overshadowed the remainder of the county, it often was given additional powers by the legislature, sometimes at the expense of the county. In Virginia, a number of cities became independent of

13. A selectman in a New Hampshire town recently rebelled against a quaint habit: "By Greenfield tradition, every selectman kept his own 'blotter book.' Into this bulky volume of 200 or so 18-inch pages my faithful predecessors had always copied the names and addresses of every resident or non-resident property owner and the size, location, and assessed value of every piece of land, every barn, house, and shed." He continued. "I felt a surge of rebellion. 'Wouldn't a single good record kept in the office serve as well as three records?' My colleagues replied that that was the way it had always been done." George Kendall, "Notes from a Selectman's Blotter Book," *Yankee* 42 (November 1978): 120.

14. See above, p. 112.

counties—that is, legally speaking they are not "within" counties (though some of them are surrounded by a single county).

Powers granted to incorporated communities varied from state to state. Even within one state, powers varied. In fact, some bills incorporating towns read like the text of a petition of a landowner who wanted to attract buyers of his lots. Some small incorporated places provided no government services at all and existed only on paper; others assumed even greater authority than their acts of incorporation granted.

Despite the disparity between the legal or practiced authority of municipalities, they often exercised functions not too different from the New England towns. The city of Wilmington, North Carolina, may suffice as an example. When the legislature in 1731 refused to charter the town on the Cape Fear River, local landowners simply laid out one anyhow and called it successively New Carthage, New Liverpool, and Newton. Within a few years there was enough activity at the place to attract the meetings of a new governor's council, the court of oyer and terminer, and the court of chancery. By the time the assembly got around to chartering the town of Wilmington in 1740, a vibrant little settlement already existed. It was not until 1743, however, that commissioners were elected and the first "town book" was started. Within two years the commissioners were adopting resolutions and ordinances suggestive of New England towns. One of their first actions was to order the keeping of a public market "under the Town house for the present until proper Shambles be built" and to require the sale of all beef, veal, mutton, venison, and pork directly to the general public for at least one hour before it was offered wholesale "so as all forestallers of the Mark[ett] may be discovered and the Inhabitants supplied at the first hand." At the same meeting James Smallwood was granted permission to build a "Piazza or Shade" at the front of his house.

From that point on, the records of Wilmington read almost as though the municipality operated independently. Through commissioners elected by the freeholders, the town (for a time called a borough) exercised broad control over the lives of its residents. It levied taxes, adopted ordinances, created offices and filled them, monitored public behavior and levied punishment on citizens who misbehaved, regulated the construction of buildings and the goings and comings of slaves, dogs, and goats, assigned citizens to work on the streets and wharfs and fined those who failed to work, provided general fire protection and required residents to sweep their chimneys every fortnight and keep handy baskets and leather buckets for firefighting purposes, regulated the quality of meats and provisions sold at the market, and maintained a public whipping post. Sample orders: prohibition of the sale of "unwholesome or stale Victuals, no Blown meat, Bulls flesh, Murrain Beef, Ram Mutton, or Leprous Swine"; prohibition of three or more slaves "playing, Riotting or Caballing on the Lords Day commonly called Sunday, or on any other day, or in the night time of any Day"; making illegal the sale of milk mixed with water; requiring that all firewood be at least four feet in length; requiring slaves to carry "tickets" signed by their owner or overseer and prohibiting them from buying or selling at the market; setting a curfew at 10:00 P.M. for slaves; and ordering that John Burgwin move his offending "necessary house or cause a vault to be sunk so as to remove the said nusance." In 1774 the commissioners ordered the construction of a "Ducking Stool"—a crude chair fastened to the end of a wooden beam extended out over the water—so that an offender could be ducked underwater in accordance with the severity of his sentence. Bakers, who were required to cook their initials into every loaf of bread, were strictly regulated; the weight and price of loaves were determined by the cost of flour. Fire precautions included prohibition against storing hay, straw, fodder, or oakum inside a building, and the burning of tar and pitch on the wharf. Lehansius Dekeyser was fined forty shillings for allowing his chimney to become so filled with soot that it caught fire; and a position of town scavenger was created to remove refuse.[15]

Wilmington was typical of hundreds—even thousands—of other municipalities throughout the land whose records reveal much about the day-to-day lives of Americans. Parkville, Missouri, for instance, adopted an ordinance requiring a license before any "organ grinders, dancing or tamborin girls, or any thing of kindred character be permitted to wander about the streets." Town records reveal that in 1858 there appeared a ventriloquist, a circus, two side shows, and two Thespian shows. In early twentieth-century Lake Forest, Illinois, it was illegal for an automobile to go through the streets unless it was preceded by a man on a bicycle carrying a light at night or ringing a bell or blowing a horn in the daytime. It was illegal for a sheepherder to drive his charges through Trenton, New Jersey, while wearing a false face. And in Tulsa, Oklahoma, kisses in public were limited to three minutes.[16] Whether implemented or not, such ordinances tell much about the customs of a community and the lives of the people.

15. Donald R. Lennon and Ida Brooks Kellam, editors, *The Wilmington Town Book, 1743–1778* (Raleigh: North Carolina Division of Archives and History, 1973), pp. 2-229 *passim*.

16. Cited in Donald Dean Parker, *Local History: How to Gather It, Write It, and Publish*

Many cities have now grown to gigantic sizes, some of them have assumed county-like powers, and all of them administer a bewildering array of programs creating vast quantities of records. Just as small-town life shows through the records of Wilmington and Parkville, matters of far wider interest may be found among records of other municipalities. An example was the "discovery" in Birmingham, Alabama, in 1978 of an estimated forty thousand documents dealing with the civil rights controversy of the 1960s, including the police department's transcript of a telephone conversation between Martin Luther King, Jr., then in jail, and his wife.[17] Historians more familiar with the record-keeping propensity of local governments should not have been so surprised to "discover" these materials among the routine documentation of the city.

It (New York: Social Science Research Council, 1944), pp. 63–65. This volume was reissued in 1979 by Greenwood Press, Westport, Connecticut.

17. "City Finds Historic Civil Rights Records" [Associated Press dispatch], *Charlotte Observer*, June 17, 1978.

8

A Brief Subject Analysis of Local Records

THE British scholar David Beers Quinn has observed that because there was no central authority in America prior to the Revolution, archival materials of the colonial period are largely local.[1] Other historians have pointed out that independence and statehood did not drastically affect the documentary responsibilities of counties and municipalities, and that while there has been an increasing assumption of authority by the state and federal governments, counties and municipalities too have taken on many additional functions. The record-making propensity of local governments, therefore, has not been curtailed significantly by the centralization tendencies of recent times.

In the following pages, local records most commonly of interest to researchers will be discussed briefly under fifteen rather broad subjects. This review is intended to be suggestive rather than exhaustive. For a more extensive listing, the serious researcher in local records will seek out recent inventories and guides prepared by local governments themselves or by state archives personnel. In the absence of more modern inventories, the researcher will find immensely useful those prepared by the Historical Records Survey of the Works Progress Administration during the Franklin Roosevelt administration. Sadly, most of these early works were issued only in mimeographed form and were not extensively preserved. Copies, however, are usually available in the state archives and in major libraries designated as depositories for federal documents. In addition to the title, quantity, location, inclusive dates, and brief description of each series of records, the HRS inventories generally incorporated a history of the county or municipality

1. David Beers Quinn, "A Chance Rag-Bag of Survivals: The Archives of Early American History," *Library Journal* 103 (November 15, 1978): 2306.

and of each agency that created records—information that is essential to an understanding of the records themselves. To be sure, some of the records listed in the HRS publications may have been relocated, lost, or destroyed under approved retention/disposition schedules; but the value of the inventories is not lessened by such actions.

Because quotations are drawn from local public records in a number of states, space will not be taken to provide individual citations to sources.

Birth, Death, Marriage, and Divorce Records

Births, deaths, and marriages comprise some of the oldest records in the country, but, paradoxically, they were among the most poorly kept until the twentieth century. Not surprisingly, New England towns more meticulously recorded and preserved vital statistics than the sprawling, sparsely populated counties of the South and West. What became habit in New England was often neglected in other areas, and the early requirement for officially recording births and deaths was dropped from the statute books in some colonies and did not reappear until early in the twentieth century. If such inattention to vital statistics appears inexplicable today, we should remind ourselves that only in our own lifetime, with the advent of social security, welfare, and extensive foreign travel, has evidence of the date and place of birth become of more than casual concern to the average American. There was simply little need for a public record to prove one's birth and parentage. The family Bible—or individual memory—sufficed.

An official record of deaths also seemed unessential, particularly if the deceased left property, for in that case the decedent's name would in due course appear in the records when the court proved the will or appointed an administrator.

Provisions for recording births and deaths have been dissimilar among the colonies and states during America's 372-year history. For example, though births were entered in the 1620s in Plymouth, Massachusetts, 299 years passed before Georgia got around to requiring general registration. In the interim there was variation from state to state and also from county to county and town to town. Some cities and counties began keeping vital statistics long before state law required their entry, and records of some New England towns were published late in the nineteenth century.

Churches, of course, often kept records of their own members, and in Alaska the vital records kept by the Russian Orthodox Church are of

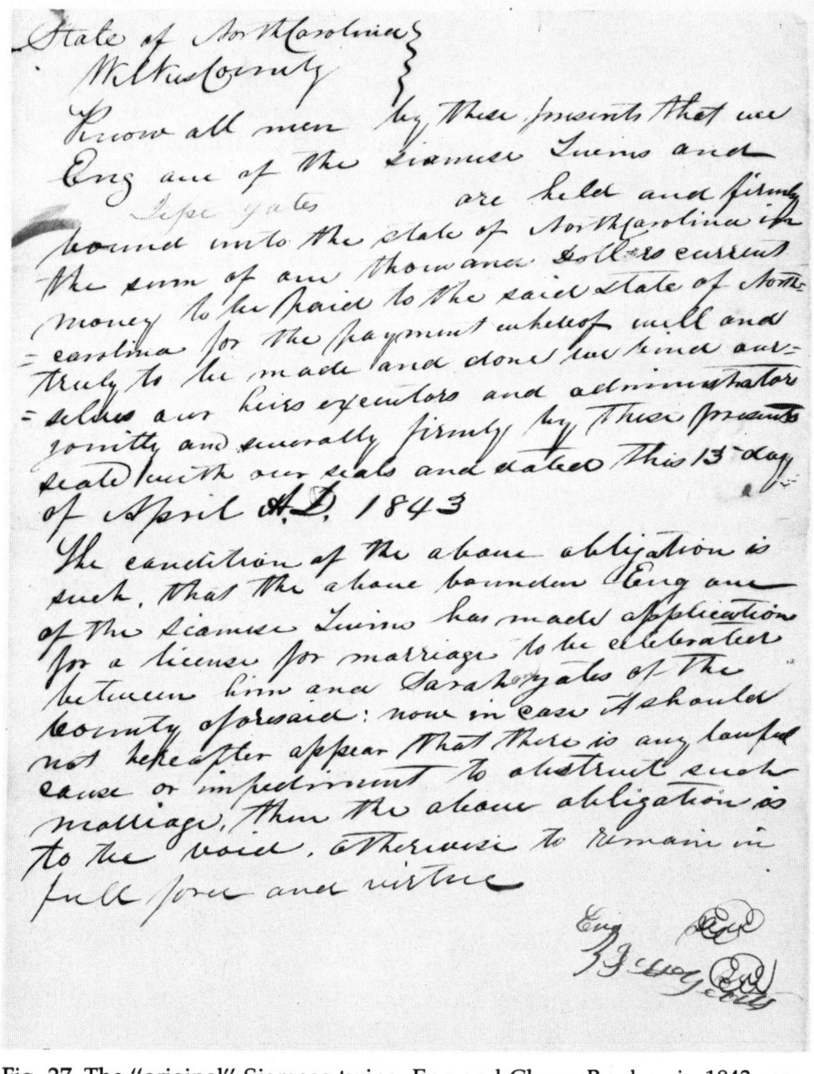

State of North Carolina }
Wilkes County }

Know all men by these presents that we
Eng one of the Siamese Twins and
Jesse Yates are held and firmly
bound unto the state of North Carolina in
the sum of one thousand dollars current
money to be paid to the said State of North=
carolina for the payment whereof well and
truly to be made and done we bind our=
selves our heirs executors and administrators
jointly and severally firmly by these presents
sealed with our seals and dated this 13th day
of April A.D. 1843

The condition of the above obligation is
such, that the above bounden Eng one
of the Siamese Twins has made application
for a license for marriage to be celebrated
between him and Sarah Yates of the
county aforesaid: now in case it should
not hereafter appear that there is any lawful
cause or impediment to obstruct such
marriage, then the above obligation is
to be void, otherwise to remain in
full force and virtue

Eng (Seal)
J. Yeates (Seal)

Fig. 27. The "original" Siamese twins, Eng and Chang Bunker, in 1843 married, respectively, Sarah and Adelaide, the daughters of Jesse Yeates who signed their almost identical marriage bonds. Eng is named here as the prospective groom of Sarah. (North Carolina Division of Archives and History)

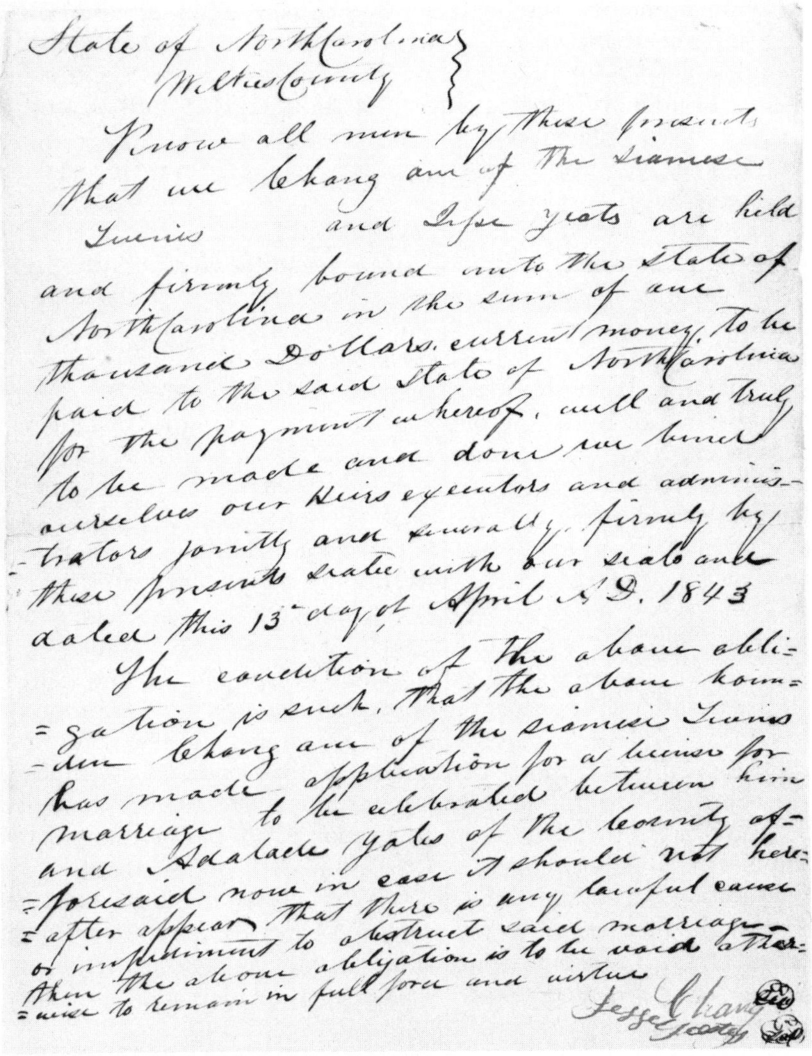

State of North Carolina }
Wilkes County }

Know all men by these presents
that we Chang one of the Siamese
Twins and Jesse Yeats are held
and firmly bound unto the State of
North Carolina in the sum of one
thousand Dollars current money to be
paid to the said State of North Carolina
for the payment whereof, well and truly
to be made and done we bind
ourselves our Heirs executors and adminis-
-trators jointly and severally firmly by
these presents sealed with our seals and
dated this 13th day of April A.D. 1843

The condition of the above obli-
-gation is such, That the above boun-
-den Chang one of the Siamese Twins
has made application for a license for
marriage to be celebrated between him
and Adelaide Yates of the County af-
-foresaid now in case it should not here-
-after appear That there is any lawful cause
or impediment to obstruct said marriage
then the above obligation is to be void other-
-wise to remain in full force and virtue

Chang (seal)
Jesse Yeats (seal)

Fig. 28. Marriage bond of Chang Bunker, named here as the prospective groom of Adelaide Yeates. Chang was the Siamese twin of Eng Bunker (Fig. 27). (North Carolina Division of Archives and History)

great importance to the state today. Traditionally, however, vital statistics have been the responsibility of local governments. In many counties, despite that tradition, the performance was poor and often depended upon the personal interest of clerks. It is not unusual to find births casually entered between wills or other recorded documents, and, in some New England towns, entries have been found mixed with land records.

In recent decades, the states have established statewide systems of registration. Normally, a birth or death record is filed with the local health department (or another local agency), which forwards a copy to a state registrar of vital statistics. Thus a record is kept both at the local and state level. In addition, microfilm copies are furnished to the federal government for statistical purposes. This modern system, however, has not corrected the problems created by centuries of carelessness or negligence, and researchers will often have to read the early unindexed records of appropriate counties and towns in hopes of finding vital records.

Birth and death records have research values beyond names, dates, and kinship. Both are particularly useful in population and demographic studies; births are of interest to nearly all shades of social scientists; and deaths provide important data for medical studies.

Marriages were recorded more assiduously than births and deaths, certainly partially because of the implications of morality and property ownership. Still, early marriage records sometimes consisted only of a bond, signed by the prospective groom, a bondsman, and a witness. The bond signified that there was no legal impediment to the marriage, but it did not prove that the wedding took place. Furthermore, early bonds usually gave the names of the couple but not of parents. Not until around the middle of the nineteenth century did official marriage licenses and registers rather universally provide fuller information such as age, kinship, date of marriage, and the officiator. Marriages, too, are now generally recorded both at the local level and in established central recording offices.

A special type of marriage record is found in some of the southern states. These are cohabitation bonds by which, following the Civil War, freedmen were allowed to legalize their common-law marriages. These little-known certificates are of considerable importance in the study of black genealogy and history.

Records of divorces are even more elusive, for traditionally court action (or sometimes an act of a legislature) was required. Records of early divorces, therefore, are usually buried in court records. Only since divorce has become a familiar occurrence have the states begun a central registration of their divorce records.

The National Center for Health Statistics has published three useful booklets, all available from the Government Printing Office: *Where to Write for Birth and Death Records, Where to Write for Marriage Records,* and *Where to Write for Divorce Records.* Though somewhat out of date now, the Historical Records Survey of the Works Progress Administration in the late 1930s and early 1940s published guides to public vital statistics in a number of states.

Wills and Estate Records

Wills and estate records provide no exception to the checkerboard character of record-keeping among local governments. What is said of one state may not be true at all of another. It is not surprising, however, that, into the eighteenth century, probate proceedings sometimes were exercised by high officials such as the governor or his council, and in those cases records were usually filed with the colonial secretary. Gradually, however, jurisdiction over the settlement of estates was assumed by the county court or a separate probate or surrogate court.

Great importance was attached to the settlement of estates, and strict procedures were followed under the watchful eye of the probate authority. Typically, a will was required to be examined by members of the court, and if found authentic, admitted to probate—i.e., registered as genuine. The court then appointed the executor, accepted his bond, received an inventory of the personal property and real estate, determined its division, required an accurate accounting by the executor, and then allowed him his fees. In the absence of a will, the court appointed an administrator or administratrix who followed somewhat similar procedures.

Prior to the twentieth century, wills were usually laboriously copied by hand into a bound book, and the other "loose papers" (bond, inventory, allotment of dower, allotment of year's provisions, annual accounts, petitions and orders, divisions, final accounts, etc.) were folded and placed in chronological order along with other estate papers. The original will was sometimes returned to the fiduciary or family; in some areas it was routinely filed. Even when the original will was kept, however, the will book constituted the reference copy and was zealously guarded by the clerk of the probate jurisdiction. In some areas, lists and accounts were also copied into books titled something like "Inventories" and "Record of Settlements." The copying of documents into bound books resulted in such infrequent access to the originals that the latter were often stored under undesirable conditions and sometimes were destroyed.

With the demise of a county court, probate authority was usually transferred to a clerk or separate register of wills. As in the case of other records, estate settlements have been more carefully recorded and maintained since the advent of the typewriter and photocopying equipment, and a recent trend has been the discontinuance of book records and the substitution of case files, each holding the will and all documentation relating to the particular estate. In many older counties, however, the earlier manuscript papers have been poorly kept and are not easily accessible even if they have been preserved. Often the book records have been microfilmed by the state, by a local agency, or by the Genealogical Society of the Church of Jesus Christ of Latter-day Saints; and film copies are increasingly available in state archives and the Genealogical Society's own library. In some states an effort has been made to centralize in the state archives the early original records, particularly the loose papers.

Wills and settlements of estates have always been a prime source for genealogists seeking family relationships. When a will does not spell out the relationship of heirs, the pattern of devises often provides reliable clues in identifying children, grandchildren, etc. Furthermore, even when the will does not name the spouse or children or when there is no will, the supplementary records—particularly the division of the estate—are likely to provide names of primary relatives (even of the disinherited who are left only one dollar). A will also may by its very wording reveal much of the condition and character of the testator. Mary Fortsen, after willing her property to her son on condition that he take care of his father, added, "Provided allwaise yt. if it shall please God to send me safely delivered of ye child I goe wth, all yet ye same shall have Equall Share with ye said Theophilus." Only in her will is there evidence that she was pregnant at the time. A century later Arthur Dobbs, nearly eighty years of age, expressed improbable hopes when he provided for his eighteen-year-old wife "and her Issue, by me Boegotten, in case she shall have any or be pregnant at the time of my Decease." James Blount left to his wife all his personal property "porvisardly that She, the Sd Elizabeth doth remain wedow, otherwaise, no longer then She the Sd Elizabeth Shall marry; at that time of her maredge to returne to my blovd Daughter, Anne." Edward Bryan asked in his will that his four children be given at least seven years of schooling "in such Siencies as the Exrs: shal think proper." Nathaniel

Duckinfield instructed that he be buried "without the least Pomp and Show, Which to me is a strange Absurd Vanity, to Tarry Death Victories over Mortals in Triumph to the Grave." He explained, "I have not studied Law Phrases but have Used Words without guile, Suitable to the Simplicity and integrity of my Own mind and With Intire Approbation of my own Reason and Consideration of things." Caleb Grainger asked to be buried in a plain black coffin and that there be purchased out of his estate for Cornelius Harnett a "neat Mourning Ring which I begg he may wear in remembrance of his Sinciear Friend & Brother." Henry Hyrne directed that his friend be permitted to purchase one of his servants, "the said Lucey having been a good Slave, it is my desire that my said friend, Frederick Jones should have her, as I am Sensible his humanity is such that he would treat her well."

Records of estates singly reveal a great deal about the status, lifestyle, and standard of living of a family; collectively they provide firsthand evidence of the economic and social conditions of an entire community. An analysis of these records over a period of time can trace the transformation of a frontier existence into a sophisticated society, cabin-dwelling farmers into slave-holding planters, penniless immigrants into industrial leaders. A similar analysis may also disclose the financial and social deterioration of a family or community. A careful study can trace the introduction of new farm implements and house furniture, the changing modes of tableware, the prevalence of jewelry or art objects, the reading habits of the citizens, the coming of the tractor and the disappearance of the mule, the domestication of animals.

Wills are important sources for the study of slavery. The disposition of slaves often dominates the wills of southern planters, and much can be learned about the individual attitudes of the testators. Freeing of slaves by will was fairly common, but also instructive are the explanations of why individual servants were left to specific members of the family. Distinctions are often drawn between field hands and house servants, between obstreperous youngsters and respected elders, between blacks and mulattoes. The pairing of slaves with other bequests—land, money, personal property—illustrates relationships of values at the time of the writing of the will.

Collectively, wills of members of a particular family or community appear as cornucopias, filled with insights into their writers. They may be studied for information on literacy (many a grand dame has been shocked to discover that a fabled ancestor signed his will with an "X"), place names (wills often give names of individual fields or houses and refer to streams and villages by earlier, now uncommon names), morals and customs (testators are prone to leave advice, particularly for errant children), and an almost infinite variety of other subjects. Perhaps this is not surprising, for a will may be interpreted as the effort of a person to continue to manage his worldly goods after his death.

Many property owners failed to prepare a last will and testament—thus they died intestate. Even so, the law required the appointment of an administrator to inventory, divide, and account for all property. Thus only the propertyless are usually absent from probate records.

Inventories of estates, accounts of sales, and final accounts are even more fertile than wills for some types of research. The minute itemization of property—down to the last cooking pot or garden hoe or suit of clothes—provides a fascinating peek into the daily lives of families. Certainly the inventory of the estate of William Bartram cannot furnish a full picture of the man, but the appearance of "1 Mouth peice to put on Negros" and "1 pair Iron hoppels for Negros" may shed some light upon slavery in colonial days. Mention of a substantial amount of pewter—thirty new and eighteen old plates, twenty-six spoons, eleven basins, and five dishes—and a wide assortment of other table and kitchenware suggests a man of substantial means, a conclusion supported by the listing of thirty-four cows and calves and "Some horses & Mairs & Some Cattle Supposed to be runing in the woods the Number Not known." Interestingly enough, when Bartram's son died, years later, the inventory of his estate also showed "1 Mouth peice for a Negro"—perhaps the same one inherited from his father. We do not know if it was ever used. William, Jr., appeared to be a physician, judging from his accumulation of "Doctor Books & Docter's Medicens & Vials & pots." The inventory of the estate of Dr. John Eustace discribed a surprisingly large library, each volume listed individually.

The richness of detail found in estates records is surprising to all but the most experienced local researcher. Fiduciaries usually took their duties seriously and listed names and property in great detail. A study of the variety of documents encompassed in the definition "estate records" will often reveal identities not only of family members but the multitude of persons who played some small role in the funeral and subsequent settlement of the estate—the preacher who officiated at the funeral, the coffin-maker and grave-diggers, the neighbors who shrouded the body, the merchant who sold the winding sheets, the distiller who furnished whiskey for the wake, the persons indebted to the deceased person and the persons to whom he or she was indebted, and the names of the fiduciary, court officials, and lawyers who handled the estate. The worldly possessions of the deceased are likewise listed individually: cows, steers, yearlings, and calves; mares, colts, horses, mules, geldings, jennies, and jacks; sows, shoats, and boars; tea pots, coffee pots, milk pots, cooking pots, and butter churns; dried pork, beef, and venison, and hog grease; hides, skins, and bones; flax wheels, woolen wheels, cotton wheels, wagon wheels; quilted gowns, morning gowns, calico gowns, chintz gowns, and cotton gowns; silk coats, claret-colored coats, bearskin coats, fustian coats, and cotton coats; clothes of all types and sizes; household furnishings of infinite variety, often listed room by room; a lengthy list of farming implements or other tools of trade; slaves by name, age, and sex.

For a study of the livelihood, worldly possessions, and family life of Americans, no record reveals so much as wills and estates records. In addition to the identification of people and property, these materials often contain the prices for which each item was sold or allowed in the equitable division of an estate. Accounts of sales also list the names of purchasers or recipients, enabling the tracing of a revered antique from one generation to another. Much of our knowledge of the arts and crafts of America comes from studies of estate records. The Museum of Early Southern Decorative Arts, for instance, has traced thousands of craftsmen through these records, and directories of craftsmen demonstrate the vast amount of data available in estate records.

Long used by genealogists to trace family lines, wills and estate records hold great potential for broader purposes of history.

Records of Orphans, Apprentices, and the Disadvantaged

Compassion is not new in America. Although there is little similarity between the institutionalized, computerized public welfare system of our day and the simple, personalized procedures of a century or more ago, there was indeed in early America a sense of obligation to the under-aged, over-aged, and the helpless—an obligation carried out by local government. Inherent in the system was the assumption that every person should make his own way in the world, but that organized society should help those who, because of age or disability, could not care for themselves. A strong work ethic discouraged abuse of the system.

Orphaned children with an estate were commonly placed under the care of a guardian designated by the court. A condition of guardianship was good character and a bond guaranteeing proper treatment of the ward and frugal handling of and accounting for that part of the estate put at the guardian's disposal. In 1762, for instance, a county court ordered that "Poll Pigg, orphan girl aged 13, shall live with John Donahoe for 3 years, he behaving to her as he does to his own children." Children over fourteen could usually choose their guardian: "David Poe orphan of Simon Poe decd. came into Court and made choice of James Massey as his Guardian, who entered into bond with George Herndon and William Howard, £1,000." Annual reports and final accounts were required of guardians, and these documents, together with the guardian bonds, furnish helpful information for many purposes. For example, every expenditure on behalf of the ward is entered, showing the purpose, amount, and payee. In no other public record is there kept such a detailed account of the cost of growing up—room, board, clothing, medical attention, education, etc. School accounts, for instance, may name the teacher, tuition costs, courses taken, and books purchased. Medical expenses may reveal a doctor's method of treatment of a particular illness, including the drugs administered. The purchase of special tools may indicate the interests, skill, or trade for which the ward was being prepared.

When minors who were not orphans came into possession of an estate through inheritance or gift, their property was also placed under a guardian for management. Care must be taken, therefore, to distinguish between orphans and other minors whose parents were still alive and together. It is also important to remember that both parents need not be dead for a guardian to be appointed for an orphan. The appointment took place when the surviving spouse could not take care of the child or was not qualified to serve as guardian.

While orphaned children with an estate were fortunate enough to be placed under a guardian, destitute orphans were not so lucky. If no relative took them in, they were usually apprenticed out—in effect, made an indentured servant until the age of responsibility. An apprenticeship indenture between a master or mistress and the court signified agreement that in return for the labor and loyalty of the apprentice, the master would provide bed, board, medical attention, and training in a trade or skill. In 1778 Elizabeth Culpepper Jackson was bound to James Sellers "until she arrives at the age of eighteen years, being now fourteen years old to learn the business of spinstress &c." In case of mistreatment, wards had recourse to the court: "Elinor McCome made complaint against her master, Wm. McDeed, that she was ill-used by him; court ordered him to post bond of £20 proc[lamation money] to insure his good behavior toward her during the remainder of her servitude." Disputes over apprentices were also settled by the court:

"Tim. Cleven brought in the mulatto boy named Antone, the court canceling his indenture to Cleven, freeing him under the conditions of his indenture in Anson County."

Parents, sometimes destitute, sometimes simply wanting their child to learn a skill and trade, could apprentice the youngster with or without an order from the court. In 1780 the Yohogania County, Virginia, court acceded to the request of Ann Hammon that her son Isaac be bound to Isaac McMichael "until he arrive at the age of 21 years being now 5 years of age, and that the sd. McMichl. teach him to read wright & cipher as far as the rule of three, also trade and Mystery of Husbandry and give him one new suit of Cloth, a Bible, Grubing how and ax, at the expiration of sd Term." But the more unfortunate were children born out of wedlock, who usually took the surname of the mother. However, bastardy was a crime, and if a mother identified the father, or if his identity was determined by the court, he was placed under a bastardy bond and required to provide for the upkeep of the child. Otherwise, the child was often apprenticed: "John Barton Howeel a base begotten child aged about 3 years, to be bound to Thos. Greer till age 18 to learn the trade of a weaver." The commitment of the master was often to provide "Good and Sufficient meat drink washing and lodging apparill and all necessarys fitting for such apprentice . . . [and] to instruct teach or cause to be instructed or taught . . . in the art of a coopers trade to make a good and merchantable barrell workemanlike." At the end of the apprenticeship the ward was to be furnished "a set of coopers tools and a good suit of apparil."

Guardians were also often appointed for the mentally incompetent and the physically disabled. In other cases, receivers were appointed to hold and manage property. In all cases, strict accounting was required, and the records are filled with data important to many types of research.

In caring for other categories of the unfortunate, early officials differentiated between "the sick and impotent and therefore unable to work" and "the idle and sturdy and therefore able but not willing to exercise any honest employment." Furthermore, they were quick to escort beyond their borders nonresident vagrants. It was expected that each county or town would be burdened with only its own human tragedy. Aid to the worthy poor took several forms. They could be exempted from the poll tax; they could voluntarily bind themselves as apprentices or servants in return for their upkeep; or they could be given direct aid—either money or, through arrangement with others, room and board. In the latter instance, the county or town contracted with private citizens who provided homes for the destitute. By the end of the eighteenth century, however, a common institution was being established: the "poor house," a place operated by the local government, where the paupers were brought together, housed, and fed. The condition of the homes and the quality of the care differed from place to place, but everywhere their character was essentially the same: publicly supported institutions for the care of those who could not fend for themselves. Too often the wardens (or overseers) of the poor had no choice but to place in the "poor houses" the mentally and physically deficient citizens who could not be cared for by their own families. Consequently, the name *asylum* was often attached to the homes.

Imprisonment for debt was fairly common in early America, and records relating to debtors are both pathetic and enlightening, for they often describe in considerable detail the nature of the debtor's obligations and the claims of his creditors. Schedules of property and accounts of sales are similar in value to the final accounts found among estate records. The records are useful also for a study of economic and social conditions during various periods.

Slaves were certainly the most unfortunate of all Americans, and documentation about them is found in almost every series of local records where slavery existed. The town records of North Castle, New York, indicate that a condition of manumission there in 1789 was that a slave be "under fifty years old and of sufficient Abilities to git his own living." Some communities required freedmen to leave the town, county, or even the state as a condition of their emancipation. Perhaps the most obvious documentation on the institution of slavery is found among the bills of sale and estate records previously discussed. In addition, however, most litigation involving slaves was handled at the county level; consequently, the court records are a prime source for a study of the behavior and treatment of slaves. For example, for burglary, two slaves received these sentences: "Scipio shall suffer Death by being Hanged and the Negro Abraham shall suffer Corporal punishment by haveing one Ear nailed to the Stocks & cut off and also shall have Fifty Nine Lashes well Laid on his bare back."

Property Records

Although proprietary and royal grants were sometimes recorded at the colony level, land recordation has generally been a local responsibility in America, except in the territories prior to statehood. Today even grants from the federal and state governments are entered locally. These records customarily formed the most voluminous body of documentation in the county, until the advent of the welfare system. Happily, there has been more standardization of land records than is characteristic of most other records, and, generally, real estate documentation is easily accessible. The explanation lies in the convenience of book records and the frequent reference required to them by grantors, grantees, and tax assessors.

The transfer of real estate requires a document normally called a deed, which, like a will, must be admitted to probate—that is, registered as genuine. Deeds were proved by county or probate courts in earlier times; now they are often examined and recorded by a local official such as a clerk, recorder, or register, usually at the county level. However, deeds are recorded by some large cities (Baltimore, for example) and towns (in Connecticut, Rhode Island, and Vermont). Alaska has registration districts, with a central office in the state capital.

Deeds (including deeds of trust, mortgage deeds, and other instruments of conveyance) were usually copied into books by hand (later by typewriter or photocopy), and the books, often brightly bound in leather and resting on expensive roller-type shelves, made the recorder's office the showplace of the courthouse. Alphabetical cross-indexes to grantees and grantors guide the searcher to the particular book and page number. In recent years some recorders have substituted microform recording, thus eliminating bound books altogether. Computerized recording systems are likely to be implemented in the larger counties within a few years.

A deed often conveys more information than the date, names of the grantor and grantee, amount of consideration, and description of the property. Although the property being transferred is registered in the county of its location, either the grantor or grantee, or both, may be living in another county or state, and that information was often indicated. Family relationships are sometimes stated, or the conditions under which the transfer was made. A deed of gift, for instance, may express appreciation for the kindness of the grantee (a daughter) who cared for the grantor in old age when no other son or daughter offered assistance. The conveyance may reveal that the property was sold to pay off a debt or to satisfy taxes, or that it was acquired under the headright system. The metes and bounds may be as intriguing as they are informative, for they may refer to long-forgotten landmarks that can be relocated by a careful processioning of the lines.

In recent times, the actual amount of money involved in the purchase of real estate is seldom given, and even in considering transactions of earlier times care must be taken in interpreting the amount literally. Usually the amount of the transaction can be determined on modern transfers by adding up the cost of the tax stamps affixed to the deed and relating it to the tax percentage then in effect.

The importance of property was relatively greater in former generations when the right to vote and hold office was limited to men who met minimum personal and/or real property ownership standards. A family's social status also tended to be commensurate with its possession of worldly goods.

Because counties have been divided from time to time, the tracing of land records back through many generations may involve the consultation of the records of four, five, or even more counties that at one time encompassed the property. In some instances, deeds for property were copied into the newly formed county's own deed books, but that procedure was an exception rather than the rule.

There are, of course, in addition to the recorder's standard deed books a variety of other records relating to property. One of the most important series is the plat books containing maps of property. Often, early deeds carried a scrawled miniature map in one corner, but in this century surveys by licensed personnel have become commonplace. These large and heavy volumes compete for space in crowded offices and, because of their chemical composition, often exhibit signs of early wear or deterioration. Additionally, there are various means of transferring interests in property, each with its own series. Ohio's county records manual lists no fewer than three dozen separate series of records that relate directly to real estate. In addition to the data in the recorder's office, information concerning land transfers may often be found in the records of civil courts where disputes were adjudicated.

The recorder often handled documentation for transfers other than of real estate. Bills of sale involving property of considerable value were routinely recorded, sometimes right in the deed books. The most common items referred to in recorded bills of sale were horses, cattle, valuable pieces of furniture, and—in the South—slaves.

The recorder's office is a repository of research materials valuable for the study of the descent of property, the average acreage of farms, the variations in land values, the migration of national and religious groups, and many other subjects. Genealogists have long used these records effectively; the materials are of equal importance to researchers with broader interests.

Tax Records

The earliest American taxes were generally poll (i.e., capitation or head) taxes, but during the passing centuries almost every conceivable method of public levy was introduced. Most of them are documented in the records of county and municipal governments.

Some settlers argued that the payment of quitrents removed any further responsibility that they might have had toward the colonial proprietors or the crown, but that medieval vestige did not protect the residents from special levies for such local purposes as construction of a courthouse or town hall. Furthermore, as county and town governments became more regularized and the population grew, these special levies became so frequent that local governments resorted to a small annual poll tax on individuals of certain ages—sometimes white males from sixteen to fifty and slaves of both sexes from twelve to fifty-five. Like everything else in the field of local records, however, standards for taxation varied throughout the country.

Though property taxes were not unknown in the colonies, it was not until during and after the Revolution that this form of taxation became widespread. Slaveowners of the South resisted the classification of slaves as property and preferred to continue paying a poll tax on each servant rather than subject such "property" to taxation by value (ad valorem). The poll tax had no relation to the right to vote until modern times, and it was, of all American taxes, the most commonly accepted means of supporting government for the first two centuries of settlement.

The poll tax was relatively easy to administer. A tax lister had but to record the names of the "tithables," as those subject to taxation were sometimes called. Occasionally, however, the tax lister favored history by indicating the age and other information on both white and black polls. If there was an unresolved question concerning age, the individual was haled before the court, which pronounced a legal age—right or wrong. The court also had the power to exempt persons from the capitation tax. Not surprisingly, the most common exemption was a slave in poor health; the relief, of course, was to the master, not the slave.

The earliest property taxes were on real estate, the standard either being quantity (acreage or lots) or assessed value. Next came luxury items such as body ornaments, silver and china, pianos, gigs, and carriages. Finally, almost all personal possessions were included—farm implements, household furniture, livestock, even pots and pans. Special taxes were levied on liquor dealers, slave traders, dentists, teachers, and many others. In fact, the tax forms utilized in one state in 1860 provided (among many others) columns for the following entries: acres of land and valuation, town lots and valuation, polls, interest, dividends, riding vehicles, dentists, lawyers, physicians, teachers, pistols, dirks, Bowie-knives, sword-canes, dirk-canes, daguerreotypists, painters, gates across highway, ferries, Negro traders, liquor dealers, note-shavers, stud-horses and jacks, plate and jewelry, gold watches, silver watches, distilleries, commission merchants, produce brokers, auctioneers, harps, and pianos. Appropriate spaces were provided, of course, for any property without its own column. In the same state, special taxes were later placed on theaters, opera houses, traveling theatrical companies, museums, performances, lotteries, pool tables, tobacco dealers, grocers, peddlers, hotels, gypsies, and fortune tellers—and many others. Sometimes extra taxes were levied on members of religious groups who refused to perform military service.

Tax records were often viewed as useless once payment had been received, and many of them were discarded. Yet, a surprisingly large quantity has been preserved, thanks in many cases to their relegation to forgotten storerooms. The surviving records vary so greatly in format and location that only a state-by-state study can reveal their potential. That they contain much information of use to researchers, however, there is no doubt. For the early colonial period, long before the initiation of censuses, lists of polls provide virtually the only comprehensive recording of names of adult males. From these lists population projections can be made, individuals can be identified in relation to their community, the extent of slave ownership can be estimated, and patterns of migration may be deduced.

Even more informative are tax records listing private property and real estate holdings with their assessed values. In these massive records are the data for gauging standards of living of individual families and of the community as a whole; for determining the relative values of different types of worldly goods; for estimating average landholdings in a community; for observing the rise and fall of property values; for dating and determining the approximate costs of buildings; for determining the impact of a depression upon the fortunes of the people; for following the fortunes of individual families or groups. Urban historians find tax records of special value in tracing the growth of cities and the attendant problems; economic historians can use tax records as a reasonably reliable gauge of economic activity; business historians have yet to exploit fully the vast amount of data available in records relating to taxes on business since the Civil War; and social historians have thus far done little with records of taxes on cultural events, amusements, and diversions. Indeed, tax records are among the most under-used documentation of local government.

Trial Court Records

Broadly speaking, court records include deeds, wills, estate papers, and other documents falling within the jurisdiction of various courts. In this section, however, reference is limited to legal issues before the court, either criminal or civil (including equity).

The jurisdiction of county and municipal courts differed widely from state to state and from one local government to another within each state. It was fairly common in the colonial era for county courts to exercise jurisdiction over noncapital criminal cases plus civil cases in which the amount at issue did not exceed a few hundred pounds. In matters involving slaves, however, the county court usually had unlimited authority, including capital punishment. As intermediate courts were established late in the colonial and early in the statehood periods, the jurisdiction of the county court was usually reduced. The establishment of these intermediate courts—often called district, circuit, or superior courts—did not necessarily remove cases from the county; in fact, these new courts periodically sat in each county and the records for a particular county were maintained in the courthouse. Thus, though a case was tried in a district court, the record was normally filed in the county where the action originated.

Only through a study of the judicial organization of a particular state and locality can the complexity of a court system be understood. The introductions to the inventories of county records published by the Historical Records Survey of the Works Progress Administration are helpful in this connection. More recently, some states have published special guides to court records. One of the most commendable of the latter is *A Report on the Records of the Minnesota District and County Courts,* published in 1978 by the Minnesota Historical Society under a grant from the National Historical Publications and Records Commission. This eighty-one-page publication is worthy of note because, in addition to retention/disposition schedules, it contains a history of the county and district courts and describes in layman's language the more than one hundred series of court records commonly found in each Minnesota county seat. Thus it constitutes a guide for users as well as a manual for local officials in the disposition of court records. Another report prepared with assistance from a grant from the NHPRC is *An Inventory and Guide to the Records of the Massachusetts Superior Court and Its Predecessors,* published in 1978 by the Massachusetts Judicial Records Committee.

Criminal cases dealt with violations of law, and charges were usually brought in the name of the state or the people—for example, "The State [or The People] *v.* John Hennessee, Indictment: Murder." Offenses ranged from petty to capital, from misdemeanor to felony. A trial may or may not have been by jury. The records created by courts handling criminal cases vary greatly, but usually there is a criminal docket or register that lists the name of the defendant, the offense, note of proceedings conducted, and summary of verdict or sentence. While this docket may serve as a sort of table of contents, the details of the case are more apt to be told in the criminal case files, which often contain warrants, subpoenas, affidavits, depositions, and other supporting materials. In addition, there are usually other series of records in which the case is entered—the minutes of the court, costs docket, fee docket, half-fee docket, etc.

The use of criminal trial records is obvious to an understanding of a particular case, but they have additional value both individually and collectively. Much extraneous information can be obtained by reading the papers. In the San Augustine County records, the bill of indictment in the case of the Republic of Texas versus Feliciano Lopez and others for treason in 1838 mentions "Bowie knives," an indication that the weapon named for James Bowie was well known only two years after his death. In Kent County, Delaware, Samuel Burbery and John Clayton were fined one shilling each "for Smoaking tobacoe in Court." In the same county, a fifteen-year-old boy "did seemingly Commit Buggery with a Mare of Isack Freeland in Mr. Frenches Pasture." The youth denied the charge "but ounes that he would have Committed buggery with her if Thomas French had not Come to him." The case was bound over to the provincial court. An angry judge in Bucks County, Pennsylvania, fined members of a hung jury for "Illegal proceedings" after they had the constable "Cast a peice of mony in his hat" for a verdict. In the same county, Gilbert Wheeler was found guilty and fined for selling rum to the Indians. In Perquimans County, North Carolina, John Clary was convicted of forcible fornication with his stepdaughter and was expelled from the state legislature, but his fellow citizens re-elected him with an even larger majority. These and innumerable other court records enliven the past and provide sources for the study of the criminal justice system in all its ramifications. A tremendous amount of legal and social (and not a little political) history lies fallow among the tons of criminal case records throughout the country.

Perhaps even more significant for the study of the past are the records of civil actions, either adversary proceedings or *ex parte* proceedings.

Adversary proceedings refer to litigation between two or more parties (e.g., "Sarah Siddons v. Moriah Miller, debt."). Most such cases involved land, estates, livestock, debt, breach of contract, or slander. Examples are legion. John Pile, Jr., brought suit against John Cashat and John Craiden for "mismarking of a Hog"; Cashat was found guilty and ordered to pay Pile ten pounds and pay an additional fine of ten pounds, and Craiden was exonerated. Jane Cloverdale, using a four-letter word not normally found in the records, accused Philip Conway of sexual assault and asked for damages. Joshua Dark sued Spier Widener for payment of a horse which Widener had overworked. Catherine Dabler sued Peter Brandon for the custody of "an Infant Girl born of the Body of the said Catherine." Alen Tharp and his wife charged that Michael Humble "did forcibly and with a Strong hand Carry away from them, the Complainants, five of their Children." Johann Wagner brought suit against his brother, Kurt, for cheating him out of his share of his father's estate. And on and on.

Ex parte proceedings involved only one party and usually consisted of a petition to the court. Common subjects were a father's petition for the legitimation of a child born before wedlock, an alien applying for citizenship, a farmer asking for assistance in ejecting an unwelcome tenant, a widow asking for a dower from the estate of her husband, a family asking for an order to divide an estate, a citizen asking for a license to operate a ferry or ordinary, a request of a master to be permitted to emancipate a slave, a petition from an indentured servant for an order to compel a master to provide adequate maintenance. Again, the variety of petitions appears infinite. For example, in Yohogania County, Virginia, Edward Ward petitioned the court to excuse him from serving as sheriff "until the line Between the States of Virginia and Pennsylvania are fixed or limited, for on the North Eastern Bounds of this County There is still a Door open for dispute and Contintion, which has been heretofore the cause of Disturbing the Peace of the People Settled and claiming alternately The Jurisdiction of each Government. . . ." Members of the court, "being of the opinion that he is no sheriff untill he enters into Bond before this Court," relieved Ward of his duties but immediately swore him in as a fellow justice of the

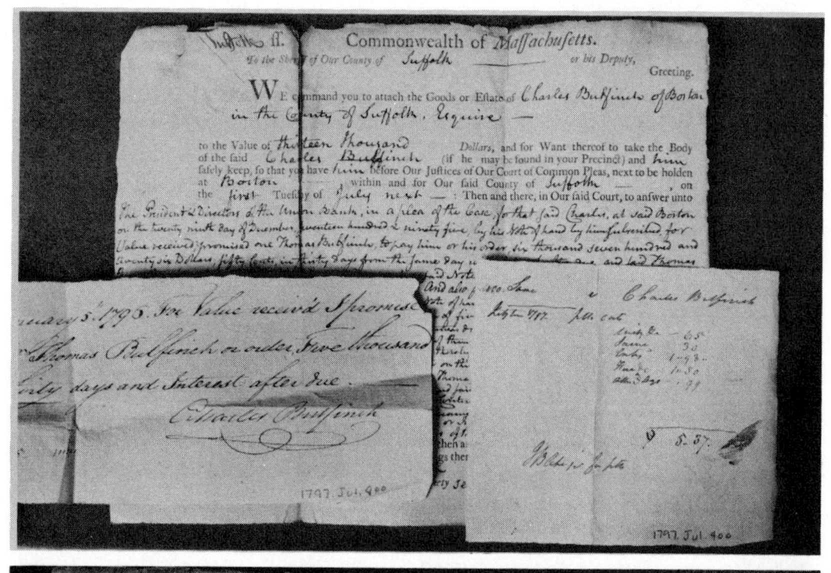

Suffolk ss. Commonwealth of Massachusetts.

To the Sheriff of Our County of Suffolk or his Deputy, Greeting.

WE command you to attach the Goods or Estate of Charles Bulfinch of Boston in the County of Suffolk, Esquire —

to the Value of thirteen thousand Dollars, and for Want thereof to take the Body of the said Charles Bulfinch (if he may be found in your Precinct) and him safely keep, so that you have him before Our Justices of Our Court of Common Pleas, next to be holden at Boston within and for Our said County of Suffolk, on the first Tuesday of July next — : Then and there, in Our said Court, to answer unto The President & Directors of the Union Bank, in a plea of the Case for that said Charles, at said Boston on the twenty ninth day of December, seventeen hundred & ninety five, by his note of hand by him subscribed, for value received promised one Thomas Bulfinch, to pay him or his order, six thousand seven hundred and twenty six Dollars, fifty cents, in sixty days from the same day [illegible] and said Thomas [illegible]

[illegible]uary 5. 1796. For Value receiv'd I promise [illegible] Thomas Bulfinch or order Five thousand [illegible] [illegible]ty days and Interest after due.

Charles Bulfinch

1797 Jul. 400

Charles Bulfinch

[illegible] 5.57

1797 Jul. 400

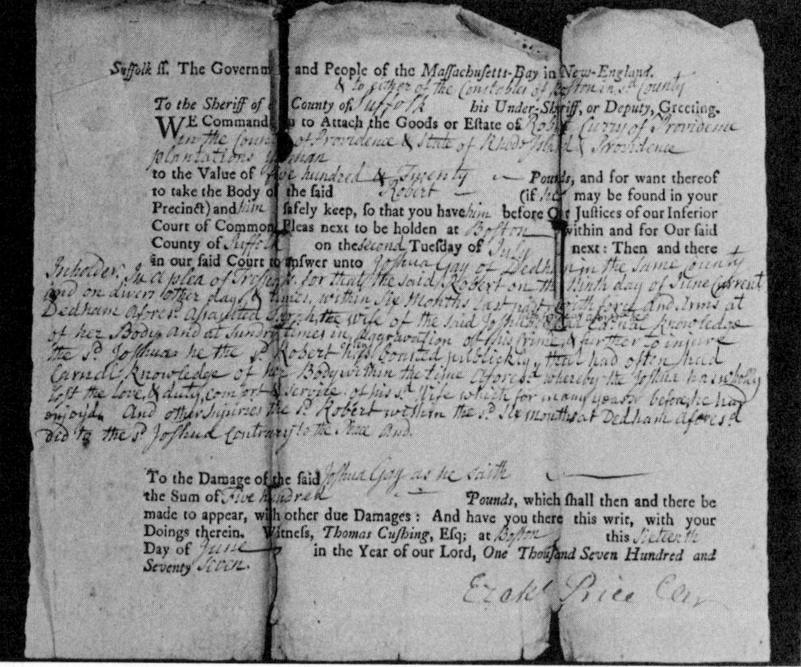

Suffolk ss. The Government and People of the Massachusetts-Bay in New-England.

& to either of the Constables of Boston in sd County

To the Sheriff of our County of Suffolk his Under-Sheriff, or Deputy, Greeting.

WE Command you to Attach the Goods or Estate of Robert Curry of Providence in the County of Providence & State of Rhode Island & Providence plantations Yeoman

to the Value of five hundred & Twenty Pounds, and for want thereof to take the Body of the said Robert (if he may be found in your Precinct) and him safely keep, so that you have him before Our Justices of our Inferior Court of Common Pleas next to be holden at Boston within and for Our said County of Suffolk on the second Tuesday of July next: Then and there in our said Court to answer unto Joshua Gay of Dedham in the same County Inholder. In a plea of Trespass for that the said Robert on the Ninth day of June current and on divers other days & times, within Six Months last past with force and Arms at Dedham aforesd assaulted Sarah the wife of the said Joshua & had Carnal Knowledge of her Body and at Sundry times in aggravation of this Crime & further to injure the sd Joshua he the sd Robert hath boasted publickly that had often had Carnal Knowledge of her Body within the time aforesd whereby the Joshua has wholly lost the love, & duty, comfort & service of his sd Wife which for many years before he had enjoyd. And other Injuries the sd Robert within the sd Six months at Dedham aforesd did to the sd Joshua Contrary to the Peace and.

To the Damage of the said Joshua Gay as he saith the Sum of Five hundred Pounds, which shall then and there be made to appear, with other due Damages: And have you there this writ, with your Doings therein. Witness, Thomas Cushing, Esq; at Boston this Sixteenth Day of June in the Year of our Lord, One Thousand Seven Hundred and Seventy Seven.

Ezekl Price Cler

Fig. 29 and Fig. 30. The Suffolk County (Massachusetts) Inferior Court of Common Pleas touched the lives of both the famed and the humble: in Figure 29, papers revealing the bankruptcy of the noted architect, Charles Bulfinch; and in Figure 30, the story of the seduction of Sarah Gay by Robert Curry. (Courtesy of Gabrielle Keller)

peace, noting that none of *them* would take on the thankless sheriff's job, either. This simple exchange in the records adds color and understanding to the local rivalries on the frontier during the Revolution. Local court records are pregnant with such revelations of the attitudes and circumstances of the people who made the American nation.

Election Records

The exercise of the quintessential American tradition of the ballot has produced at the local government level a rich assortment of records that have been ignored by genealogists and seldom exploited by scholars. Although many of these records for earlier periods have been discarded, a surprisingly large quantity can still be found in courthouses and town halls, and others have been transferred to state archives.

Naturally, the types and formats of election records vary from place to place and from time to time. Early returns tended to be on scraps of paper; later, considerable pains were taken to copy abstracts of the returns in bound books or onto forms, though standardization was slow in coming. One or more of the following series will be found in local governments that have preserved some or all of their elections records:

Registration books, which list each registered voter by precinct, name, address, age, race, and recently by party affiliation. Sometimes these books also give birthplace, occupation, former residence, reason for deletion of name from the rolls (death, removal out of the precinct, convicted felon, etc.), and proof of payment of poll taxes. Registration books may yield information useful in biographical studies, but more importantly they may be used to analyze political parties in relation to their membership's economic or social status, national origin, race, geography, etc. Compared with other censuses of residents, the registration books also reveal some of the effects of voting qualifications in the days when the suffrage was limited.

Poll books, which indicate who actually voted in each election. These records, if preserved, may be compared with the registration books to determine the interest or apathy of the electorate in exercising its privileges.

Minutes and administrative records of the elections board, generally of recent origin, which deal with drawing election districts, establishing polling places, appointing and monitoring activities of election officials, investigating charges of irregularities, and other administrative matters. Records of investigations of alleged irregularities sometimes reveal the influence and methods of political leaders and organizations.

Financial statements of candidates, also of recent origin, which may include an identification of the sources of all receipts. By comparing reports of two or more candidates, a researcher may establish the affinity of particular candidates with ideologies and issues. Expenditures may illustrate changing strategies in the race for votes—for instance, the shifting of advertising from newspapers to television.

Abstracts of election returns, which list the countywide or townwide votes for each candidate for each office. This is the "official" return—the permanent record. For elections involving district, state, or federal offices, a copy of the abstract is usually sent to the state elections officer (in recent times, local elections boards furnish also a copy of returns for local offices to the state elections agency). The abstracts are the records most frequently used by researchers, because they tend to be convenient. They do not, however, normally contain precinct breakdowns.

Precinct returns, from which the abstracts are prepared. Surviving precinct returns are both rare and valuable, for they provide a precinct breakdown of the vote for each candidate. It is from these records—often merely tally sheets, in earlier times—that researchers may follow voting patterns down to the smallest political unit.

In several southern states are found three especially important series of registration books. The first consists of lists prepared in 1867, before freedmen were admitted to the suffrage. The next consists of lists prepared in 1868 under military rule and following the extension of the suffrage to freedmen. This second series is immensely valuable in the study of black history for the information that it contains; it is also valuable in the study of whites for the information that it does not contain, for thousands of whites were disfranchised, and their names do not appear in the 1868 registers. The third series consists of "permanent registration books" prepared after the adoption of the "Grandfather Clause"—constitutional amendments that, by means of a literacy test, again disfranchised most of the blacks while providing that illiterate white men could be registered if a direct ancestor had been registered in 1867. These latter two series may be found at the local level or sometimes among the records of the secretary of state.

These and other series of election records may have been carefully preserved in one county or town, but in the neighboring community they may not exist at all. Samuel P. Hayes found fairly complete voting returns, tally sheets, and precinct poll lists dating from 1817 in Harrison

County, Indiana, but in the adjoining Floyd County the election records had been disposed of when the county government moved into a new courthouse.

Surviving election records may be located in several different departments of local government, for there was no clear pattern of responsibility until the establishment of local boards of elections in the past century or so. In some instances voting records have been consolidated in the board of elections, another local office, or the state archives. Researchers will need to refer to an existing inventory of records, or, if no inventory has been prepared, inquire of officials such as the clerk and register.

Election results, including county-by-county totals, have been published for statewide and national races in some states, but these printed figures are not always accurate. For years, figures were published showing that North Carolina voted for the Whig candidate in the presidential election of 1852 when, in fact, the original returns and the official certification showed that the state gave its electoral votes to Franklin Pierce. Recently, archivists and historians have assisted in the compilation of voting statistics for the Inter-University Consortium for Political Research in Ann Arbor, Michigan. These figures, which are computerized by the ICPR, are usually based on the abstracts of returns filed with the secretary of state, though in many cases newspaper reports were accepted. Still, the researcher wishing to analyze voting patterns at the precinct level must depend upon the precinct or voting district returns kept at the local level.

Military and Veterans' Records

Military and pension records are normally associated with the central government, but they may also be found at the local level, especially among eighteenth- and nineteenth-century county records.

The militia was composed of adult free males except ministers, physicians, ferrymen, millers, public officials, and some other groups who often were exempted from service. Counties provided a regimental commander—a colonel—under whom captains, representing districts, in turn commanded men of lesser rank. Officer status was a mark of distinction and was much sought after. In peacetime the militia protected the county against Indian attacks (or sometimes initiated attacks upon the Indians), put down slave uprisings and riots, protected the court during sensitive trials, assisted citizens in times of disaster, and generally provided a reliable back-up force in case of need. In times of war, the militia could be called up for state or even national service. Militia musters were often colorful occasions, combining training, discipline, and pleasure—almost a county-fair atmosphere, particularly attractive to politicians. Muster rolls and a variety of ancillary records may be found in many counties. For instance, one of the very first actions of the Dutch court of Wildwyck, New York, in 1661 was to observe that while there was no grain available for the militia, Pieter van Alen, the shoemaker, was exporting wheat. Upon deliberation, the court ruled that "the Shoemaker shall deliver his remaining grain to Sergeant Christiaen Nissen romp."

Captains' districts sometimes provided a convenient subdivision for taxing purposes, and not infrequently tax lists are arranged according to these designations.

Armed forces discharges have been recorded in many counties, and some counties and towns have kept rosters of their men who went off to war. These records, while seldom complete, furnish at least a partial roster of men who served from a particular area, along with the service record of each. Such records were usually handwritten, or, more recently, typed, photostated, or microfilmed. Some have been published.

It was not uncommon for a destitute or disabled Revolutionary War veteran (or his widow) to be exempted from local taxes, and county and town records sometime explain in considerable detail the veteran's military contributions and his property holdings. In addition, applications for federal pensions for war service were often made through county officials, and these records provide interesting data on each applicant. For instance, in Stokes County, North Carolina, Noah Bailey's application showed that he fought in the battles of Brandywine, Germantown, Monmouth, and Guilford Courthouse, and was wounded in the left hip at Eutaw Springs; his worldly goods consisted of no real estate and only "1 sow & pig, 2 beds & furn, 4 chairs & little h. h. furn worth ca $40.00." With these meager possessions he had to support a wife and "a fitified dau[ghter]."

Some states authorized special county commissions to provide for the welfare of veterans. In Ohio, for instance, the Soldiers Relief Commission originally was concerned with helping indigent Union veterans and their families, but subsequently the commission extended its concern to veterans of other wars. Among its records are minutes, individual case files, and burial records.

Because the federal government provided no pensions for Confederate veterans and their widows, that task was left to the southern states. Applications filed through local officials provide not only a great deal of information on the individual veterans but also accompanying affidavits often give interesting (if sometimes exaggerated) accounts of battles in which the applicants participated. Some of the most vivid accounts of military encounters are found among pension records.

Transportation Records

Although the states have increasingly taken over the cost and control of highways, that was traditionally a local duty, and in some states local governments still are responsible for all but major highways. Early records relating to the laying out, construction, and repairing of roads are among the most interesting and informative documents found at the county and municipal level.

At first, roads were the responsibility of the individual settler, but it soon became evident that by combining their efforts neighbors could provide improved paths and cartways with perhaps less individual labor. As settlement expanded, the need for community action increased, and soon county courts, town boards, or special road commissions assumed the authority to direct owners to organize themselves into road companies responsible for the building and upkeep of specified sections of a public way. One substantial resident was appointed supervisor, overseer, or surveyor of roads for his area, and able-bodied men were required to donate their labor and implements for a specified period of time each year. Failure to work led to a fine. For example, this entry is found in the seventeenth-century records of Charles County, Maryland: "Clement Thompson . . . for refuseinge to assist in the mendinge of the highways (beinge drunck & not able to answer for himselfe) is fined 100 lb. tobacco." Thus the first public roads in America were built not by taxes but by the hands of those who used them.

In addition to the lessons about community effort and construction techniques, petitions and orders for roads teach much about settlers and early landmarks. Better than perhaps any other record, these documents place individual residents in relation to their neighbors and to other places commonly known at the time but soon lost to history. This entry in county court minutes is an example:

> The Petition Sundry of the Inhabitants of this County was Read Praying the Liberty of a Cart Road from the Old Main Road Near Newbys Mill to a place on Vosses Creek for a Publick Landing. . . . Beginning at the Old main Road near to where a School House was formerly burnt opposite Joseph Newbys

fence and from thence the most Direct way to Joshua Guyers to the place called Old Schooner Landing where the Petitioners & others are to have the benifit of a Publick Landing. . . .

The road overseer and his neighbors were responsible for building the roads, causeways, and bridges under primitive conditions. In one colony, an act of 1715 required that

. . . all publick roads . . . shall be cleared of and from all Trees & Brush at least Ten Feet wide & such Limbs of Trees cut away as may incommode horsemen travelling that road. All Bridges or Causeways made or to be made over Swamps or small Runs of Water the pieces wherewith the same shall be made shall be laid athwart the road & at least Ten foot long well secured & made fast & covered with Earth & all Bridges over Deep & navigable streams shall be made at least ten foot wide with sufficient and strong pieces of plank at least Three Inches thick with firm & strong Post & Bearers well secured and fastened.

Standards for road construction rose dramatically over the decades, but the responsibility of citizens to construct and maintain highways by their own hands was generally accepted until the Civil War. There were some exceptions, however, in the cases of major arteries. In addition, some private corporations were chartered for the construction of toll roads. In the 1850s, for instance, hundreds of miles of toll plank roads were constructed. Individuals, too, could build toll roads or bridges by obtaining a license and paying taxes on their gates.

The potential of road records to elucidate history is substantial. For example, by comparing the early road records with maps, wills, deeds, and other town records, the historian of New Castle, New York, was able to superimpose the town's present highway system on a 1797 map with striking results: most of the present highways follow closely the roads laid out nearly two hundred years ago. Found among the records of the town were detailed maps of various roads, showing residences, businesses, and landmarks, plus an 1845 map of the plans to extend the New York and Harlem Railroad through New Castle.

Ferries, ditches, canals, public landings, and wharfs were also often the responsibility of local governments, and county and town records may be found relating to them. Once ferry landings were prepared, operation was usually carried on by a ferry keeper whose license required him or her to provide service during specified hours at rates set by the local government—for example, "Ordered that Fanny Berry have leave to keep a ferry over Haw river near Redfield ford and that her rates be . . . for a Man and Horse 1 shilling."

Public transportation facilities are not entirely new, for late in the nineteenth century some municipalities established horse-drawn (and later electric) streetcar transportation. Where these were operated by the municipality, records may have been preserved detailing their financial and physical operations. In some parts of the country, local records will be found relating to riverboats and river dredging, ocean-going vessels and ports, canals and canal boats, railroads, stage-coaches, automobiles, and airplanes.

Records relating to roads and means of transportation include petitions, reports of road juries, orders for surveys, appointments of overseers, lists of fines for failure to work, contracts and performance bonds, financial records, routes and schedules, and papers relating to litigation over roads and transportation. These records may be found in a variety of offices. For instance, in the South they are likely to be among the clerk's records, whereas in Ohio the likely repository is the county engineer's office.

Naturalization Records

Like military records, documentation relating to aliens and naturalization is normally associated with the federal government. However, prior to 1906, naturalization proceedings, unless conducted in a federal court, were required to be conducted in a lower court of record. Furthermore, after that date when a federal agency took over the function, many of the newer records also remained in the custody of local courts. The two-step naturalization process included, first, a declaration of intention to become a citizen and renouncement of former allegiances, followed some years later by a petition for and court order actually granting citizenship. Some immigrants never took the final step, often on the assumption that the declaration was sufficient. Researchers, therefore, may find records of declarations even more useful than the subsequent court orders granting citizenship.

Naturalization records are especially important, for they often provide considerable personal data, including the name of the applicant, address, age, place of birth, number of years in America, occupation, names of relatives—in fact, a biographical sketch. Several years ago one of North Carolina's favorite legends—that a country school teacher, Peter Stewart Ney, was actually Marshal Michel Ney, who had escaped a French firing squad in 1815—was effectually destroyed when the records of Lancaster County, South Carolina, yielded the naturalization of the same Peter Stewart Ney, a native of *Scotland*.

School Records

Public schools were virtually a monopoly of New England until the nineteenth century, and records relating to education vary greatly from place to place. Because of the local nature of early education (some states had thousands of small school districts), the proportionately few surviving records may be found in the hands of successor consolidated school districts, in the state archives, or even in private hands.

School records usually consist of the following:

Minutes of the board of education or common schools which, in addition to providing identification of members of the board, school officials, and teachers, describe school district boundaries; location, construction, and upkeep of buildings; qualification for admission and rules of student behavior; and statistics on attendance. The minutes, often in book form, may be supplemented by petitions and contracts.

Student rosters or school censuses, listing the names of students by age, sex, level of attainment, and parents or guardian.

School registers or pupil records, repeating much information from the student rosters but also indicating attendance record, courses taken, grades, and behavior. Some of these records may contain a list of teachers for the various grades or courses, titles of textbooks, names of school committee members, and information on extracurricular activities.

Personnel and budgetary records, containing data on terms and salaries of school teachers, receipts and disbursements, school tax rates, and maintenance and operating of the schools.

Records of superintendents whose activities created records concerning inspection, finances, salaries, certification of teachers, and related matters.

Lucky is the county or municipality that has preserved the records of its public education system, for the story of education in America has not been fully told. The surviving records are rich in untapped data both for biographical use and for the broader study of public education.

Records of Coroners' Inquests

Long before the creation of the office of medical examiner, a citizen of each county served as a coroner (originally *crowner*) to investigate and, if necessary, conduct inquests over violent and mysterious deaths. In some places, the coroner substituted for the sheriff when the latter officer was incapacitated. Ideally, the coroner was a physician, but there were no physicians in many counties, and the position was filled by another citizen, qualified or not. Often a coroner's jury assisted in making a ruling.

Coroners' records are among the most fascinating records to be found, not so much for their morbidity as for their indicativeness of the great variety of causes of violent deaths over the centuries. Elizabeth Knott was murdered by an Indian wielding a lightwood knot; Elizabeth Jones's death resulted from an assault by her husband using "a Large Halter and a great Knott on One End"; Judith, a slave, died from "Hardness of the Weather and Lyquor being in Her"; William Lock drowned in a puddle of water through "an Axcident Permited by God"; William Peacock was "Murthered by one of his Negroes which was Try'd & Condmd. and Burnt at a Stake"; David Jamison died after a two-bout fight (verdict: "chance—medley"); James Jones died from "Over drinking and lying in the Road In the Sun, the liquer working in him"; and Marey Padgit was killed by "the unResistabell vapor and force of thunder and Lightning." Some coroners' certifications were more a commentary on the attitudes of the community and times than on the cause of death. For instance, in Iredell County, North Carolina, in 1878, Jule Davidson, a black man who had confessed to a murder, was seized by a lynch mob and left hanging for three days beside the railroad. When finally the coroner went to view the body, he discovered that the sheriff had taken it down and buried it. Without exhuming the corpse, the coroner ruled that Davidson "had come to his death at the hands of unknown parties." The entire community, of course, knew exactly who the "unknown parties" were.

Powers of Attorney

Powers of attorney are legal instruments authorizing a person to act as the agent or attorney of a grantor, and they often provide proof of relationship between a person's former and subsequent residence. The documents also often identify members of a family who may be living in other parts of the country. The records, which include the names of grantor and grantee, authorization to act in specific situations, notarization, date filed, and clerk's name, were usually entered in the recorder's office. These documents have considerable potential, particularly in genealogical research, and they may also be useful in studying migration patterns.

Grand Jury Records

The quality of grand jury records varies greatly, often depending upon the seriousness with which the chairman carried out his responsibility. Because the grand jury is both accusative and inquisitorial in authority, its findings are of great importance. It may initiate investigations on any matter that it desires, whether or not a violation of the law is suspected. In Minneapolis a grand jury in 1921 asked the city council to require licenses for establishments that sold soft drinks, because some of them, according to the jury, were actually fronting for prostitutes. Grand juries are best known for their investigations into organized crime, but their findings in relation to the general administration of government and of justice often lead to remedial action, either through administrative, judicial, or political means.

Records of Corporations

Counties often kept records of corporations and partnerships operating within their borders. At minimum, these records gave the name, purpose, and list of officers of corporations; in some instances they contained a copy of the articles of incorporation and list of stockholders. Not all corporations were business in nature; some were educational, cultural, or charitable institutions.

Partnerships were usually business in nature, and their entries were sometimes in books titled "record of persons doing business under an assumed name" or simply "record of partnerships."

Records of corporations and partnerships are especially useful in identifying business activities and leaders and, coupled with tax and other local records, may provide a fairly broad picture of the economy of a community.

Additional business records may be found among court records, both in connection with litigation and bankruptcy proceedings.

9

Researching Local Government Records

Preliminary Study

THE records discussed in the previous chapter are among the most useful local materials for the purpose of research, but they constitute only a portion of the total body of documentation in the possession of county and municipal governments in the United States. Most of the series mentioned have obvious value for genealogy and local history. But scores of lesser-known series also have potential value for research. The impossibility of listing them all in a book this size may be illustrated by the facts that the county records required 259 pages for listing and comment in the *Ohio County Records Manual,* more than 350 pages in the Texas County Records Inventory Project's publication on Nueces County, and nearly 1,800 pages in the Historical Records Survey report published by the North Carolina Historical Commission.

Among the other potentially useful records found in counties or municipalities are jury lists, lunacy records, loyalty oaths, chattel mortgages, sidewalk and street assessments, bonds and correspondence of officials, registers of professionals, records of strays, permits to carry weapons, patrollers' reports, surveyors' records, personnel records, special proceedings, census records (locally conducted, or copies of the federal or state censuses), and financial records of great variety, including contracts. Files often yield surprises. Court case files, for instance, may contain bank records, merchants' account books, minutes of organizations, and maps of contested real estate. The author once found two rather unusual "records" in court files: a long-bladed knife used to slit a man's throat, and a kidney stone used to prove disability.

Unless only specific, highly selected bits of information are desired, a serious researcher must go beyond the heavily used records such as court minutes, estate records, and vital statistics. To know which records may contain useful information, why and how they were created, where they are located, how to approach them, and how to understand their contents, a researcher needs to study three types of materials.

1. A knowledge of state and local history and government is essential to an understanding of the records. Consequently, the best available general materials on these subjects should be reviewed. Information out of context often loses its original meaning, for words mean different things to different generations, and false conclusions can be drawn by researchers who apply modern stereotypes to earlier words and terms. A number of examples may suffice. A farmer often called himself a planter, his estate a fortune, his small farm a plantation, and his tiny unpainted house a mansion house or manor house. The birthplace of Archibald Debow Murphey was named "Murphey's Castle" because the small structure had a full second floor—the first in that area of North Carolina. In some parts of the country, certain respected citizens assumed or were given unofficial, honorary titles, such as colonel, though they were never in the militia or armed forces. Comparisons, too, differ from place to place and time to time. A farm of four hundred acres might be considered large in Connecticut but modest in Virginia; near New Orleans, a "large slave holder" might be one with a hundred blacks in bondage, while in the mountains of north Georgia a man so described might own but ten slaves. The point is that only by knowing something of the history, society, and government of an area being researched can one fit the verbiage of an earlier time into today's concepts. This is best achieved by prefacing documentary research with a general study; only then can the specific data uncovered in research be fitted intelligently into a general and broader picture. The reading of a good state history and a dependable local history will facilitate research for the amateur; a more thorough study of the literature may be expected from the professional researcher.[1]

It is important that a researcher know the "genealogy" of the county or municipality whose records are to be used. As has been pointed out earlier, boundaries change, over the years, and although the location of a particular place may be fixed, the local government

1. The most comprehensive bibliography of county histories is probably Marion J. Kaminov, editor, *United States Local Histories in the Library of Congress: A Bibliography*, 4 vols. (Baltimore: Magna Carta Book Company, 1975). Supplements will be issued from time to time. Some states have published even more complete bibliographies of county histories, including those not in the Library of Congress. The availability of such bibliographies can be determined through the appropriate state library.

having jurisdiction over it may have changed several times. Some states have published extensive information on the evolution of their counties, and these are helpful in planning one's research.[2] An understanding of the administrative history of the governmental unit is also required of the serious historian who wishes to pursue research across agency lines.

The best approach to researching local history is *from the general to the specific:* start with a broad understanding of national and state history, then turn the telescope upon the history of the community. At that point the microscope replaces the telescope, and the researcher, like the scientist, proceeds to discoveries (or rediscoveries) in the records. The new information makes sense if it can be understood in context. Although the recommended approach for research is from the general to the specific, local history should be written *from the specific to the general.* The findings, if they are worthy of general knowledge, are meaningful if presented in the larger context of regional and state history. In good local history, the curtain does not fall at the borders of the county or municipality. This is not to denigrate the individual bits of new information that make good reading in articles in newspapers or genealogical and local publications; rather, it is to suggest that the influence of one's findings tends to be far greater and more rewarding when they are fitted onto a larger canvas likely to be viewed by specialists at the state and national levels of history. State historical journals, no matter how rigorous their standards, welcome well-written articles that shed important new light upon local history. And, encouragingly, in the past few decades the more respected genealogical magazines have devoted more space to articles that have an appeal beyond the tracing of family lines.

2. A researcher inexperienced in the use of local government records should study basic guides to local history and genealogy. Unfortunately, there is no one satisfactory guide to these subjects, and the novice is faced with an increasing number of books whose titles overpromise. The field is too broad, local governments and their records are too diverse, and the laws and traditions among the fifty states and

2. An example of that type of publication is David Leroy Corbitt, *The Formation of the North Carolina Counties, 1663–1943*, rev. printing (Raleigh: State Department of Archives and History, 1969). An outline of the descent of counties in all the states is found in Ronald Vern Jackson and Gary Ronald Teeples, editors, *Encyclopedia of Local History and Genealogy. Series I, Volume I: U.S. Counties* (Bountiful, Utah: Accelerated Indexing Systems, 1977). Unfortunately, the bibliographical listings in this book are disappointing.

thousands of communities are too varied to be coherently encompassed in one published discussion, even if someone spent a lifetime trying to summarize them.

Although it devotes only a few pages to local government records, Thomas E. Felt's *Researching, Writing, and Publishing Local History*[3] is a splendid introduction to the subject and is recommended to professionals as well as amateurs. Philip C. Brooks's *Research in Archives: The Use of Unpublished Primary Sources*[4] is a short but perceptive introduction to manuscript materials, whether public or private.

There is a plethora of books by and for genealogists, but too many of them exhibit something less than a systematic approach to research. The family tree, instead of the story of the past, tends to be the objective of too many of these works. An exception is the short, businesslike approach of Carolynne L. Wendel, *Genealogical Research: a Basic Guide.*[5] Still one of the more interestingly written books on genealogy (attuned to New England) is Gilbert S. Doane, *Searching for Your Ancestors: The How and Why of Genealogy.*[6] Other books of value to beginning researchers in family history include F. Wilbur Helmbold, *Tracing Your Ancestry: A Step-by-Step Guide to Researching Your Family History;*[7] Val D. Greenwood, *The Researcher's Guide to American Genealogy;*[8] and Norman E. Wright, *Building an American Pedigree: A Study in Genealogy.*[9] Each contains a bibliography of additional works on the subject. *Black Genealogy,*[10] by Charles L. Blockson, is a perceptive guide to black family history.

3. When available, descriptive inventories of and guides to the records of a county or municipality should be studied before one begins a research trip. Public records have little in common with books that contain a table of contents, an introduction, a story, and an ending (and sometimes an index). Records were not written for the researcher. They contain entries required by law or custom—entries that are often unrelated to each other except in form. The responsibility for keeping a particular series of records varies from place to place and time to time.

3. (Nashville: American Association for State and Local History, 1976.)

4. (Chicago: University of Chicago Press, 1969.)

5. Technical Leaflet no. 14 (Nashville: American Association for State and Local History, 1969). This leaflet was also bound into *History News* 24 (June 1969).

6. Fourth edition (Minneapolis: University of Minnesota Press, 1973; New York: Bantam Books, 1974).

7. (Birmingham: Oxmoor House, 1976.)

8. (Baltimore: Genealogical Publishing Company, 1973.)

9. (Provo, Utah: Brigham Young University Press, 1974.)

10. (Englewood Cliffs: Prentice-Hall, 1977.)

The types of records preserved in a New England town are far different from those kept in a parish in Louisiana or a city in California. In short, familiarity with the records in one's own community does not assure familiarity with the records in a community in another state. The wise researcher, therefore, will learn as much as possible in advance about the records of a local government and the administrative histories of the various offices.

Unfortunately, relatively few counties and municipalities have produced through their own efforts descriptive inventories of their records. Still, an early step in plans to conduct searches in local government records should be the location and studying of any listing, description, or guide to the records. A few state archival agencies have prepared individual inventories of records in counties or municipalities; these may be only available in typed form, but they are usually available for study either at the state archives or at the courthouse or town hall. At some cost, photocopies may be procured. In the absence of individual county or municipal inventories, the chances are better that there has been compiled at the state level a general records listing for county and/or municipal records.[11] A number of these have been mentioned in this book, particularly county records manuals incorporating listings of records commonly associated with each local office.[12] Finally, field work was completed in the early 1940s in 90 percent of the American counties by the Historical Records Survey, and more than six hundred volumes of county and municipal records inventories were published.[13] As out of date as these published

11. For example, Morris L. Radoff, Gust Skordas, and Phebe R. Jacobsen, editors, *The County Courthouses and Records of Maryland. Part II: The Records* (Annapolis: Maryland Hall of Records Commission, 1963). Such inventories usually indicate when particular records exist in languages other than English. In San Miguel County, New Mexico, for instance, one will find the "Libro de Prosedimentos de la Corte de Pruebos Condado de San Miguel," the original Spanish recordings of probate court proceedings. Many of the early records of the Southwest are in Spanish and English. The "Cahier's Record" (conveyances), "Hypotheques" (mortgages), and other early records of Assumption Parish in Louisiana are handwritten in Spanish, French, and English.

12. For reference to a number of these, see chapter 2, footnote 6, and Appendix A, pp. 181–191.

13. A catalogue of the HRS publications will be found in Sargent B. Child and D. P. Holmes, compilers, *Checklist of Historical Records Survey Publications.* Works Progress Administration Technical Series, Research and Records Bibliography no. 7 (Washington: Works Progress Administration, 1942 [reprinted; Baltimore: Genealogical Publishing Company, 1969]). The HRS inventories "attempt to do more than give merely a list of records—they attempt further to sketch in the historical background of

inventories are, they still provide immensely helpful guides for the use of records in localities without more current descriptions. Inventories do not contain the records content that a researcher seeks, but they contribute to an efficient plan of study, for they enable the researcher to approach busy public officials or archivists with intelligent questions or requests that save time, encourage mutual respect, and result in pleasant and often productive research visits.

If no type of inventory of the records is available, the researcher may have to resort to brief state-by-state reviews that are not always reliable. For instance, Noel C. Stevenson's *Search & Research*[14] is not as up to date as its publication date implies, and it contains errors of both omission and commission. Nevertheless, it does include a useful if outdated bibliography and a listing of offices in which are located records of heavy genealogical use. Other guides, such as *Birth, Marriage, Divorce, Death—On the Record,*[15] whose subtitle explains that it is a directory of 288 primary sources for personal and family records in the United States, may be helpful, though, as in the case of this title, the attempt to summarize information for all states is not entirely successful.

Conducting Research

Most local government records remain in the custody of the counties and municipalities that created them. Consequently, research in the records normally is conducted in the courthouses or town halls. Inasmuch as very few local governments have established an archives, most of the extant records are still in possession of the offices of origin. Typically, there is no one person responsible for—or even familiar with—all the records of a particular county or municipality. Therefore, as pointed out previously, a researcher should have studied available inventories of or guides to the records before arriving at the courthouse

---

the county or other unit of government, and to describe precisely and in detail the organization and functions of the government agencies whose records they list." Researchers are advised to study the extensive administrative histories that precede the listing and description of the specific records. *Inventory of the County Archives of Arizona, No. 12. Santa Cruz County* (Phoenix: Arizona Statewide Archival and Records Project, 1941), p. iii.

14. (Salt Lake City: Deseret Book Company, 1977.)

15. (Rye, New York: Reymont Associates, 1977.) As its title suggests, E. Kay Kirkham's *A Handy Guide to Record-Searching in the Larger Cities of the United States* (Logan, Utah: Everton Publishers, 1974) is useful in identifying repositories of research materials, both public and private.

or town hall. A well-prepared researcher may in fact know more about the holdings of a particular office than a newly elected or appointed official. On the other hand, an interested and experienced local official may know his or her records in remarkable detail.

The reception awaiting researchers is unpredictable. Public officials, busied by the red tape and daily demands of their current recording responsibilities, usually have little time to devote to locating, delivering, and supervising the use of the older records. Their attention may be entirely occupied in making, registering, or filing current records, and the service counter may be crowded all day. Furthermore, most offices are hard-pressed for space, and accommodations for researchers may be nonexistent.

In such circumstances, a visiting researcher may represent a considerable burden to county or municipal record keepers. The welcome awaiting a researcher is likely to be cordial if the visitor exhibits good humor and advance preparation by asking intelligent questions. The degree of co-operation is often determined by the cordiality of the initial contact. This is not to suggest that local officials are naturally unco-operative; it is to emphasize that their primary duty normally does not include waiting on historians and genealogists, and the researcher should be aware of that from the outset. Woe be to the visitor who, on first meeting the records custodian, launches into a long story on his or her ancestors or research problem. Far more successful will be the researcher who states very briefly the purpose of the visit and asks for the records to be searched. Public officials respect the value of time, and they are likely to respect a researcher who wastes little time in getting to work.

To be sure, there are offices in which the custodians are not always busy, and there are many fine local officials around the country who are genuinely interested in the details of the research going on in the county or municipal building. Especially in small towns and rural counties, officials may be delighted to have visiting historians and genealogists and may enjoy suggesting other sources of possible value. This warmness should by all means be accommodated. It is always best, though, to begin a research visit in a businesslike manner, recognizing that the local custodian is paid by the taxpayers primarily to record and file today's papers rather than to dig out those of a century or more ago.

Fortunate is the researcher who happens upon a county or municipality which has an archivist on the staff, for one of the functions of an archivist is to make the documentation available for use. Even so, it is a rule of thumb that up to 80 percent of an archivist's time is spent in arranging, describing, and otherwise preparing the records for study, and there is little time left to assist a researcher. It is the duty of the archivist to make the records available; it is the duty of the historian or genealogist to do his or her own research.

In several states, the early records of research value have been centralized in the state archives or in regional repositories. This centralization generally lessens the expense of research trips and encourages wider use of local records. However, unless the central repository also has microfilm copies of the records that are required to be kept in the county or municipality (such as deed books), a visit to each community may still be required. Before starting on a research trip, one should determine whether there has been a centralization of the local records in the state to be visited.[16] Many state archival agencies have published at least a flyer indicating in general their holdings of local records; some have published detailed inventories of county and municipal records in the state archives or regional repositories.[17]

A few states have permitted public records to be transferred to nonpublic custody, such as a local historical or genealogical society or library. Even if the historical society does not physically hold county or municipal records, the local historian may provide advice and assistance to a researcher, and advance inquiry is helpful.[18] Certainly an officially designated local historian ought to be given the *opportunity* of assistance, unless the brevity of the trip or the simplicity of the search make contact impractical.

There is a cardinal principle that every local history or genealogical researcher should know: *detailed research cannot be conducted by mail.* Furthermore, it should not be conducted by mail, even if it could be. Inherent in historical scholarship is a discipline that requires the study of all available sources bearing upon the question before the historian draws conclusions. Selective information is inadequate. For instance,

16. A general statement concerning the location of county and municipal records will be found in the *Directory of Archives and Manuscript Repositories, 1978* (Washington: National Historical Publications and Records Commission, 1978).

17. An example is *Guide to Research Materials in the North Carolina State Archives: Section B: County Records,* 6th rev. ed. (Raleigh: Division of Archives and History, 1978).

18. Titles and addresses of local historical societies may be found in Donna McDonald, compiler and editor, *Directory of Historical Societies and Agencies in the United States and Canada,* 11th ed. (Nashville: American Association for State and Local History, 1978). Genealogical organizations are listed in Mary Keysor Meyer, editor, *Directory of Genealogical Societies in the U.S.A. and Canada,* 2nd ed. (Pasadena, Maryland: Libra Publications, 1978).

while one's name, kinship, and place and date of birth, marriage, and death may be obtained from indexed sources, the real character of a historical figure is more apt to be told in the many records for which there is usually no index or extensive description—civil and criminal court files, school records, tax delinquency books, powers of attorney, chattel mortgages, records of road overseers, and the like. The *real* person is thus hidden among masses of records that will yield their secrets only to the assiduous researcher.

This means that the individual who needs access to county and municipal records should travel to the source—to the courthouses and municipal buildings of America (or, if local records have been centralized, to the state archives and regional repositories). This is a harsh reality, particularly to the aged and disabled who often develop interest in genealogy and local history. For the fortunate few who can afford to hire a researcher, names can usually be suggested by the local historical society or by the state archivist.

This is not to say, of course, that specific information and copies of easily found documents cannot be requested by mail. It is appropriate to point out again, however, that the time of public officials is required to *make* the records, and few of them have much time left to search the records and write letters to researchers. Still, many types of data can be obtained by mail, provided the inquiry is addressed to the correct office, furnishes sufficient facts to make possible a check of the appropriate indexes, asks for specific information, and is accompanied by a legal-size, stamped, self-addressed envelope.[19] Increasingly, record offices are swamped by genealogical inquiries, some of them obviously of the scatter-gun type, forcing hard-pressed officials to resort to form-letter replies explaining that they do not have the staff to permit the detailed search requested.

Like an introductory conference with a public official, a letter should be brief and to the point. Two types of requests are deadly to their purpose: the one that asks for "all the information you have" on a subject, and the one that shares the writer's genealogy or research problem in great detail. Because of the limitations of indexes, a request for a copy of a will, estate record, deed, or birth, death, or marriage record should give the full name of the subject (including any variations in spelling) and the approximate date. Many marriage registers, for example, are arranged by year, then roughly alphabetically by the

19. Some record custodians believe that an inquirer thoughtless enough not to enclose return postage does not deserve an answer. That attitude can be understood when it is recalled that some offices receive hundreds of letters each week.

name of the groom. Without the approximate date, the registrar is not likely to have time to make the search.

Fees for copies of records differ from place to place. Experienced researchers have learned that enclosing a check, whether or not in the exact amount charged for copies, often speeds the request. At minimum—even if the check has to be returned for a new one—the inclusion of a check assures the public official of the seriousness of the request.

Conclusion

Neither the management of public records nor research in the massive quantities of local records is simple, and in some respects the needs of public officials and researchers may appear to be in conflict. The record makers are concerned with current problems. A tax assessor, for example, is responsible for the keeping of an accurate roll of taxpayers, assuring that assessments are fair, sending out tax notices, and recording payment. A clerk of probate is engaged in recording wills, issuing letters testamentary and other orders, enforcing the laws regarding the settlement of estates, and seeing that these settlements are properly entered in the records. Neither the tax assessor nor the clerk of probate is deliberately creating records for future researchers; yet, they are not unaware that their current records may some day be the object of great historical interest. This awareness, however, does not dictate their daily work, for they are judged by the taxpayers on their efficiency in carrying out their primary responsibilities.

Researchers too easily judge these public officials on the condition of their ancient records and upon their ability to produce historical records upon request. Such a judgment places too much responsibility upon busy officials by visiting upon them the neglect of dozens, perhaps scores of predecessors who also labored under their own current demands with too little time to care for records inherited by them. The problem faced by thousands of local governments—that of adequately caring for their archival records—has thus grown with time. It will be solved only by the implementation of such archival and records management programs as advocated in Part I of this book. For that reason, historians and genealogists ought to be in the forefront of any movement to encourage counties and municipalities to establish modern records management programs.

If this book has shown empathy for public officials, the reason is this: The author, a historian who has used county and municipal records under a variety of adverse conditions, has also worked for many years with public officials in attempting to develop improved programs of records management. This experience has yielded a lesson that ought to be more universally understood: that the interests of record custodians and historians are really not in conflict. The former make and accumulate records for future historians; historians search the records made and accumulated by past public officials. Each deserves not only the respect, but also the appreciation and support of the other.

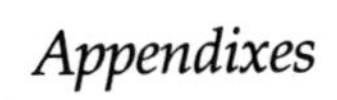
Appendixes

Appendix A

Local Records Services of State Agencies

ALABAMA

Department of Archives and History, Montgomery 36104, must approve disposition of municipal records; County Records Commission (in care of the department) prepares schedules, gives assistance in files management, and approves disposition of county records. Permanent records normally remain in the county or municipality, but the Department of Archives and History will accept them when a political subdivision cannot adequately provide for its archives.

ALASKA

State-level approval is not required for disposition of borough records (Alaska has no counties). State Archives, Department of Administration, Juneau 99811, furnishes records management advice on files management and design of records systems, and will, under limited conditions, accept permanent records for preservation in State Archives. The Alaska Municipal League in 1976 published *Municipal Records Management Program.*

ARIZONA

Department of Library, Archives and Public Records, 1130 North 22nd Avenue, Phoenix 85009, must approve disposition of county and municipal records; the department also furnishes advice on files management, design of records systems, and selection of materials, and accepts for preservation in the State Archives local records of permanent value. The department in 1977 published *Guide to Your Arizona Statewide Records Management Center.*

ARKANSAS

Arkansas History Commission, 300 West Markham Street, Little Rock 72201, must approve disposition of county and municipal records; the commission also gives advice on files management, design of systems, and selection of materials. Permanently valuable local records normally remain in the county or municipality.

CALIFORNIA

California is without a comprehensive public records act or program for local records. While disposition of many specific series of records is governed by statute, others may be disposed of by local authorities. Reluctantly the California State Archives, 1020 O Street, Sacramento 95814, will accept for preservation local records of permanent value. About a dozen repositories for local records have been established or designated under an act that authorizes county historical records commissions.

COLORADO

Division of State Archives and Public Records, 1313 Sherman Street, Denver 80203, must approve disposition of county and municipal records; the agency also gives advice on files management, design of records systems, microphotography, and selection of materials, and accepts for preservation local records of permanent value. Department of Administration, Division of Central Services, 1525 Sherman Street, Denver 80203, will microfilm local records on a fee basis. The Archives in 1976 published *Guidelines for the Preservation and Disposition of Public Records*.

CONNECTICUT

Department of Archives and Records Administration, Connecticut State Library, 231 Capitol Avenue, Hartford 06115, must approve disposition of municipal records (counties have been abolished); the department also establishes binding retention/disposition schedules, requires every town to have a fireproof vault or safe and to use permanent recording devices and materials, gives advice on files management, design of records systems, microphotography, selection of materials, and facilities security, and accepts for preservation local records of permanent value. The department in 1978 published *Records Retention Schedules for Local Governments*.

DELAWARE

Bureau of Archives and Records, Division of Cultural Affairs, Dover 19901, must approve disposition of county and municipal records; bureau also prepares schedules, provides microfilming of local records on a fee basis, and accepts for preservation in the State Archives local records of permanent value.

FLORIDA

Division of Archives, History and Records Management, Department of State, Tallahassee 32304, must approve disposition of county and municipal records; the division also gives advice on files management, design of records systems, microphotography, and selection of materials, and provides microfilming services to local governments at cost. Local records of permanent value are accepted for preservation in State Archives. Several pamphlets on legal requirements for records have been published.

GEORGIA

State Records Committee, Georgia Department of Archives and History, Atlanta 30334, must approve disposition of county and municipal records; the department also advises and trains local personnel in files management, design of records systems, microphotography, and selection of materials, and microfilms local records of permanent value. Original records generally remain at the local level, but in unusual cases the State Archives will accept permanent records for preservation.

HAWAII

Hawaii has no comprehensive records act or statewide program for local records. Inexplicably, the state comptroller must approve disposition of records that have been microfilmed, but nonmicrofilmed records may be destroyed with only local approval. Most functions characteristic of mainland counties are performed by the state, and the State Archives, Iolani Palace Grounds, Honolulu 96813, preserves many of the permanent records.

IDAHO

Idaho State Historical Society, 610 North Julia Davis Drive, Boise 83706, must be given an opportunity to accept for preservation in the State Archives any county and municipal records proposed to be destroyed. The society also advises on selection of materials and prepares retention/disposition schedules.

ILLINOIS

Local Records Commission, Illinois State Archives Building, Springfield 62756, must approve disposition of county and municipal records. Field representatives of the State Archives regularly visit local officials and assist in preparation of disposal applications. Permanently valuable local records are accepted in six regional repositories under agreement with State Archives (Northern, Southern, Eastern, and Western Illinois State universities, Illinois State University, and Sangamon State University). A pamphlet, *Local Records Act and Local Records Commission Regulations,* has been published.

INDIANA

Local records proposed to be destroyed must be approved by the County Commission of Public Records and the Archives Division, Indiana State Library, 140 North Senate Avenue, Indianapolis 46204; financial records must also be audited by the State Board of Accounts. The Archives Division gives advice on design of records systems, records scheduling, and microphotography, and provides limited microfilming of local records. Permanent local records approved for disposition may be acquired by local historical societies meeting certain criteria or by State Library. The division has published *Guide for Preservation and Destruction of Public Records.*

IOWA

Iowa is without a comprehensive records act or local records program. However, under a pilot project partially funded by NHPRC, the Iowa State Historical Department, Des Moines 50319, in 1978 began inventorying and preparing retention/disposition schedules of records of twelve counties.

KANSAS

Kansas State Historical Society, Memorial Building, Topeka 66612, and the appropriate district court must approve disposition of county records; no state approval is required for disposal of municipal records. Upon request, the society advises local officials on records problems. Some permanently valuable local records have been accepted for preservation in the society's Division of Archives, but the absence of a comprehensive records act hampers preservation efforts, especially among municipalities.

KENTUCKY

Department of Library and Archives, 851 East Main Street, Frankfort 40601, must approve disposition of county and municipal records; the department's Division of Archives and Records provides consultative services on files management, microphotography, and other records management matters, and provides microfilm and repair services on a fee basis. The department prepares retention/disposition schedules and accepts for preservation in the State Archives local records of permanent value. Several publications of interest to local officials have been issued.

LOUISIANA

State Archives and Records Service, P.O. Box 44125, Baton Rouge 70804, must approve disposition of parish and municipal records; the service also provides advice on files management, design of records systems, microphotography, and selection of materials, and local records are microfilmed on a fee basis. Some schedules have been prepared, and small quantities of permanently valuable local records have been accepted in the State Archives and in the Department of Archives of Louisiana State University Library.

MAINE

County Records Board and Municipal Records Board, both chaired by the State Archivist, Maine State Archives, Augusta 04333, must approve the disposition of county and municipal records, respectively. The State Archives provides advice on microphotography, selection of materials, and restoration services, and microfilm services are extended to municipalities on a fee basis. Local records of permanent value are accepted for preservation in the State Archives. Both boards have published *Regulations for Disposition*.

MARYLAND

Archives Division, Hall of Records Commission, Annapolis 21404, must approve disposition of county and municipal records, and retention/disposition schedules have been adopted. The commission's Records Management Division provides records management services, including microfilming. The Hall of Records accepts for preservation local records of permanent value, and all county records dating prior to 1788 must be transferred to the Hall of Records. A *Records Management Manual* was published in 1978.

MASSACHUSETTS

Division of Public Records, Office of the Secretary of the Commonwealth, One Ashburton Place, Boston 02108, must approve disposition of county and local records; the division also gives advice on files management, microphotography, selection of materials, and facilities security, and prepares retention/disposition schedules. Records of permanent value normally remain at the local level, although the State Archives accepts selected materials from county offices.

MICHIGAN

Michigan History Division, Department of State, Lansing 48918, must approve disposition of county and municipal records; the division also, as time permits, prepares retention/disposition schedules and gives advice on files management, design of records systems, microphotography, and selection of materials. Local records of permanent value are accepted for preservation in the State Archives and five regional repositories (Western Michigan, Central Michigan, Michigan Technological, and Oakland universities, and the Detroit Public Library). *Microfilm Handbook: Michigan Local Government* has been published.

MINNESOTA

Records Disposition Panel, Division of Archives and Manuscripts, Minnesota Historical Society, St. Paul 55105, must approve disposition of county and municipal records. The Records Management Division, Department of Administration, 333 Sibley Street, St. Paul 55105, as time permits gives advice on files management, design of records systems, and selection of materials. Local records of permanent value are accepted for preservation in the Division of Archives and Manuscripts and in some regional research centers.

MISSISSIPPI

Mississippi Department of Archives and History, Box 571, Jackson 39205, should approve disposition of county and municipal records. The state has no comprehensive records act or records management program, but the department does microfilm permanently valuable county records. Original permanent records are accepted for preservation in the State Archives.

MISSOURI

Local Records Board, Records Management and Archives Service, Office of Secretary of State, P.O. Box 778, Jefferson City 65101, must approve disposition of county and municipal records. The service has adopted retention/disposition schedules that are published in the *Missouri Municipal Records Manual* and a series of manuals for various county offices. Records of permanent value are retained in the local offices.

MONTANA

Local Government Services Division, Department of Community Affairs, Helena 59601, must approve disposition of county and municipal records. Montana has no comprehensive records act or program for local government records, but legislation is expected to be introduced in 1979. The State Archives, Montana Historical Society, Helena 59601, will accept permanently valuable local records, though it is customary for them to remain in the county or municipality.

NEBRASKA

Records Management Division, Office of Secretary of State, P.O. Box 94921, Lincoln 68509, and State Archives, Nebraska State Historical Society, 1500 R Street, Lincoln 68508, jointly must approve disposition of local records. The Records Management Division gives advice on design of records systems, microphotography, and selection of materials, and (with review by State Archives) prepares retention/disposition schedules. The State Archives provides selective microfilming of important local records at no charge and accepts for preservation original records of permanent value.

NEVADA

Division of State, County, and Municipal Archives, Office of Secretary of State, Carson City 89710, should approve disposition of county and municipal records. Within its limited means, the division gives advice on files management, design of records systems, microphotography, and selection of materials; it also microfilms important local records on a fee basis and accepts permanently valuable local records for preservation in the State Archives.

NEW HAMPSHIRE

Municipal Records Board, Division of Records Management and Archives, 71 South Fruit Street, Concord 03301, must approve disposition of local records. The division also gives advice on files management, design of records systems, microphotography, and selection of materials. Records generally remain at the local level, but the division will accept permanently valuable local records for preservation in its State Archives/Records Center as space permits.

NEW JERSEY

Bureau of Archives and History, New Jersey State Library, 185 West State Street, Trenton 08625, must approve disposition of county and municipal records. The bureau also gives advice on selection of materials and microphotography, and microfilms local records on a fee basis. Records generally remain at the local level, but the division will accept permanently valuable county and municipal records for preservation in the State Archives.

NEW MEXICO

State Records Center and Archives, 404 Montezuma, Santa Fe 87501, must approve disposition of county and municipal records; it also gives advice and training on files management, design of records systems, microphotography, and selection of materials. Permanently valuable county and municipal records remain at the local level, though territorial records are accepted in the State Records Center and Archives. A *County Records Manual* and a *Records Retention and Disposal Schedule for Municipalities* have been published.

NEW YORK

New York State Archives, Cultural Education Center, Albany 12230, must approve disposition of most local records, though the statutes vary according to particular classes of records. The Archives also gives advice on files management, design of records systems, microphotography, selection of materials, and facilities security. Permanent records normally remain at the local level, though a few have been accepted in the State Archives. Several publications, including retention/disposition schedules for various classes of records, have been issued.

NORTH CAROLINA

Division of Archives and History, Department of Cultural Resources, 109 East Jones Street, Raleigh 27611, must approve disposition of county and municipal records. The division also gives advice on files management, design of records systems, microphotography, and selection of materials, and repairs and microfilms permanently valuable local records at no cost. Permanently valuable county and municipal records no longer required at the local level for administrative purposes are centralized in the State Archives. A *County Records Manual* and a *Municipal Records Manual* have been published.

NORTH DAKOTA

North Dakota has no comprehensive records act or program for local records, but proposed disposition of county and municipal records should be referred to the Records Management Division and the State Historical Society, Bismarck 58505. The division gives advice on retention/disposition and microphotography. Records normally remain at the local level, but the society will accept important records for preservation in the State Archives.

OHIO

Approval for disposition of local records must be obtained from the County Records Commission or City Records Commission in the particular county or municipality, then from the Auditor of State, Columbus, after which the Ohio Historical Society, Columbus 43211, has sixty days during which it may select records for transfer to one of eight American History Research Centers. The society also gives advice on microphotography and selection of materials, and on a fee basis microfilms county and municipal records. A *Local Government Records Manual* and *Ohio County Records Manual*—the latter containing retention/disposition schedules—have been published.

OKLAHOMA

Oklahoma has no comprehensive records act or program for local records, but the Archives and Records Division, Oklahoma Department of Libraries, 200 N.E. 18th, Oklahoma City 73105, gives limited advice on records problems and will, under unusual circumstances, accept permanently valuable county records for preservation in the State Archives.

OREGON

Archives Division, Office of Secretary of State, 1005 Broadway, N.E., Salem 97310, must approve disposition of county and municipal records. The division also gives advice on files management, design of records systems, microphotography, and selection of materials, and microfilms local records on a fee basis. Records customarily are retained at the local level but in unusual circumstances are accepted for preservation in the State Archives. The published *Oregon Administrative Rules, Chapter 166: State Archivist* contains general retention/disposition schedules for local records.

PENNSYLVANIA

County Records Committee or Local Government Records Committee, Pennsylvania Historical and Museum Commission, Harrisburg 17120, must approve disposition of county and municipal records, respectively (except for Philadelphia, Pittsburgh, and Scranton). The commission's Division of Archives and Manuscripts gives limited advice on records management and prepares retention/disposition schedules for publication by the two committees. Local records of permanent value are accepted for preservation by the State Archives or by a regional repository approved by the Archives.

RHODE ISLAND

Rhode Island State Library, Providence 02903, must approve disposition of municipal records; the Rhode Island Supreme Court must approve disposition of court records (the only county records). The state has no comprehensive program for local government records, but the State Library may requisition permanent records not being properly cared for.

SOUTH CAROLINA

South Carolina Department of Archives and History, Box 11669, Columbia 29211, must approve disposition of county and municipal records. The department also gives advice on files management, design of records systems, microphotography, selection of materials, and other phases of records management, and microfilms permanently valuable local records at no cost. Local records of permanent value are accepted on a selective basis for preservation in the State Archives.

SOUTH DAKOTA

Archives Resource Center, Records Storage Building, Pierre 57501, should approve disposition of county and municipal records. The Office of Records Management gives advice on files management, microphotography, and selection of materials, and microfilms local records on a fee basis. Local governments normally retain their permanently valuable records, but they may be accepted for preservation in the Archives Resource Center.

TENNESSEE

Tennessee State Library and Archives, 403 7th Avenue, North, Nashville 37219, must be notified of proposed disposition of county records and given ninety days in which to acquire records of permanent value; in case of municipal records, the State Archives must be given fifteen days for such selection. Respectively, the County and Municipal Technical Advisory Services, Nashville 37219, provide advice on files management and design of records systems, and prepare (with approval of the State Archives) retention/disposition schedules. The State Archives microfilms permanently valuable county records to 1900 at no cost.

TEXAS

Archives Division, Texas State Library, Austin 78711, should approve disposition of all county and municipal records. The division also gives advice on microphotography and records scheduling, and microfilms permanently valuable local records on a fee basis. Permanent original records are accepted for preservation in the State Archives or in twenty-one Regional Historical Resource Depositories. The Texas County Records Inventory Project, North Texas State University, has published many inventories, and the State Archives has published *Texas County Records Manual* containing retention/disposition schedules.

UTAH

State Records Committee, Utah State Archives and Records Service, State Capitol, Salt Lake City 84114, must approve disposition of county and municipal records. The Archives also gives advice on microphotography and selection of materials, and microfilms at no cost important local records. Original records of permanent value are accepted for preservation in the State Archives. A statewide *Records Retention Schedule 1978* has been published.

VERMONT

Public Records Advisory Board, Public Records Division, Department of Administration, Montpelier 05602, must approve disposition of county and municipal records. The division also gives advice on design of records systems and microphotography, and microfilms important local records on a fee basis. Records normally remain at the local level due to shortage of space in the State Archives.

VIRGINIA

Archives and Records Division, Virginia State Library, 12th and Capitol Streets, Richmond 23219, must approve disposition of county and municipal records. The division also gives advice on files management, design of records systems, microphotography, selection of materials, and computer-microfilm interface, and microfilms important local records at no cost. Local records of permanent value are accepted for preservation in the State Archives.

WASHINGTON

Local Records Committee, Division of Archives and Records Management, Department of General Administration, Olympia 98504, must approve disposition of county and municipal records. The division also gives advice on files management, design of records systems, microphotography, and selection of materials, and microfilms important local records on a fee basis. Permanently valuable local records are accepted for preservation in the State Archives or three regional repositories (Eastern, Central, and Western Washington universities). A *Local Government Records Workshop Handbook* and other booklets have been published.

WEST VIRGINIA

West Virginia has no comprehensive records act or program for local records. The Records Management Division, West Virginia Department of Finance and Administration, Charleston 25305, prepares suggested retention/disposition schedules and gives limited advice on local records problems. Records of permanent value are accepted for preservation in the Archives and History Division, Department of Culture and History, Charleston 25305.

WISCONSIN

State Historical Society of Wisconsin, 816 State Street, Madison 53706, should approve disposition of county and municipal records. The society also on request consults with local officials on records problems and accepts for preservation in its Archives or in thirteen Area Research Centers local records of permanent value. The State Microfilm Laboratory, 4638 University Avenue, Madison 53705, provides microfilming services for important local records on a fee basis.

WYOMING

State Records Committee, Wyoming State Archives, Records Management, and Centralized Microfilm Division, Cheyenne 82001, must approve disposition of county and municipal records. The division also gives advice on microphotography and records appraisal, and microfilms important local records on a fee basis. Records of permanent value are accepted for preservation in the State Archives.

Appendix B

Selected Sources of Information on Archives and Records Management

Society of American Archivists
330 South Wells Street, Suite 810
Chicago, Illinois 60606

National Association of State Archives and Records Administrators
P.O. Box 7216
Atlanta, Georgia 30357

Association of Records Managers and Administrators
P.O. Box 281
Bradford, Rhode Island 02808

Institute of Certified Records Managers
P.O. Box 89
Washington, D.C. 20044

American Association for State and Local History
1400 Eighth Avenue, South
Nashville, Tennessee 37203

Office of Records Management
National Archives and Records Service
Washington, D.C. 20408

National Historical Publications and Records Commission
National Archives and Records Service
Washington, D.C. 20408

National Micrographics Association
8728 Colesville Road
Silver Spring, Maryland 20910

American National Standards Institute
1430 Broadway
New York, New York 10018

National Association of Counties
1735 New York Avenue, N.W.
Washington, D.C. 20006

National Association of County Recorders and Clerks
1735 New York Avenue, N.W.
Washington, D.C. 20006

International City Management Association
1140 Connecticut Avenue, N.W.
Washington, D.C. 20036

International Institute of Municipal Clerks
160 North Altadena Drive
Pasadena, California 91107

National Center for State Courts
300 Newport Avenue
Williamsburg, Virginia 23185

American Association for Vital Records and Public Health Statistics
Department of Health and Environment
Forbes Air Force Base, Building 740
Topeka, Kansas 66620

Association for Health Records
School of Medicine
Case Western Reserve University
Cleveland, Ohio 44106

American Medical Record Association
John Hancock Center, Suite 1850
875 North Michigan Avenue
Chicago, Illinois 60611

Committee on Uniform Crime Reports
℅ International Association of
Chiefs of Police
11 Firstfield Road
Gaithersburg, Maryland 20760

Traffic Records Committee
℅ National Safety Council
444 North Michigan Avenue
Chicago, Illinois 60611

Information and Records Management
250 Fulton Avenue
Hempstead, New York 11550

Index